The
Search for the
Pink-Headed
Duck

The Search for the Pink-Headed Duck

Rory Nugent

HOUGHTON

MIFFLIN

COMPANY

BOSTON

1991

For information about permission to reproduce selections from
this book, write to Permissions, Houghton Mifflin Company,
2 Park Street, Boston, Massachusetts 02108.

Library of Congress Cataloging-in Publication Data

Nugent, Rory.
The search for the pink-headed duck / Rory Nugent.
p.   cm.
ISBN 0-395-50552-6
1. India — Description and travel — 1981-   I. Title.
DS414.2.N84   1991   90-43656
915.404'52 — dc20   CIP

Printed in the United States of America

AGM 10 9 8 7 6 5 4 3 2 1

To William F. Gunkel and his crew aboard the Air Force plane that located me shipwrecked in the mid-Atlantic. Thank you, gentlemen, and thank you, Jim Angell, for laboring on the manuscript, acting as guide, editor, craftsman, and, above all, friend.

Contents

Introduction

The five of us were talking about lost treasures that night, sitting around and trading stories. What's still out there to find?

"India is the place," Jim suggested. "One of us should go after the pink-headed duck. It hasn't been sighted in years. Extremely rare . . . the most elusive bird in the world."

The next day I went to the library and found several books that mentioned the bird, last seen fifty years ago in India. One book had a picture of the duck, and I stared at it for quite some time, dreaming, imagining myself learning its song. The image stayed in my mind; no matter where I was or what I was doing, the notion of searching for the lost duck was more interesting.

Two months later, my apartment sold and everything else in storage, I took a cab to Kennedy Airport and flew to India. What follows is the story of my search for the pink-headed duck as I recall it. I took notes throughout the journey, but I soon learned that imagination was the key to finding the prize.

Giant rhododendron forest
and home of
Abominable Snowman

S I K K I M

Attempt to enter Tibet

Mt.
Kanchenjunga

H I M A L A Y A

B H U T A N

In the Himalayas

Ganju
Lama's
Home

Gangtok

A step over the border
and into Bhutan

Darjeeling

A S S A M

With the Gurkhas

Pengkhua

B I H A R

B r a h m a p

Dhubri

Bong Country

Gauh

Storm

B A N G L A D E S H

M E G H A L A Y A

DART
STUDIO

PAKISTAN

BHUTAN

TIBET

CHINA

NEPAL

Brahmaputra River

INDIA

BURMA

BANGLADESH

Arabian
Sea

Bay
of
Bengal

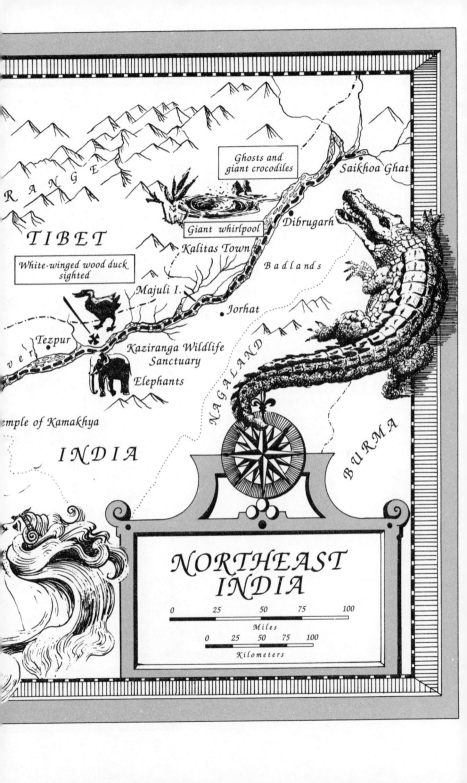

I

The Calcutta Fowl Market

IN THIS CITY where street signs are as rare as trees, I need some information. I've been wandering about Calcutta for a day and a half looking for a pink-headed duck, but the only people who will talk to me are shop owners and hucksters trying to sell me something. Then, by chance, I happen upon the Calcutta Tourist Office.

Inside a kettle boils atop a stove, and the smell of Darjeeling tea scents the air. Three men in *dhotis* shuffle behind brooms, whisking them in a tired rhythm. The officials behind the reception desk appear preoccupied as they thumb through stacks of paper. As I touch a guidebook, a large man lifts his gaze to my face. His drooping jowls and double chin bury the knot of his tie.

"Do you need help?" he asks in an indifferent voice.

"I sure do."

He nods, reaches into his coat pocket, and hands me a business card. His name is printed in Hindi and English but appears impossible to pronounce. I decide to call him "Sir."

He motions for me to sit as I unfold a city map, the best one I could find. Yesterday, while searching bookstores, I discovered that maps of Calcutta are surprisingly inaccurate, missing streets, out of scale, and improperly oriented. Locals joke that the maps are a strategic ploy engineered by the army to confuse invading Pakistani generals.

"Ah, here we are," the official says, puncturing the map, obliterating lower Park Street with the tip of his pencil.

He proceeds to point out the usual tourist attractions, which are all clearly marked: the Botanical Gardens, Howrah Bridge, Victoria Memorial, Calcutta Museum, and other places that hold little appeal for me. Finally he asks where I want to go.

"Well, Sir, I'm trying to find the fowl market."

He swallows hard and tugs a jacket button.

I repeat my request. He looks even more surprised. Shaking his head disapprovingly, he grabs a legal pad.

"Name," he demands, narrowing his jet-black eyes.

"Excuse me?"

"Name and passport." He's breathing heavily now. I hand over the document.

"Why do *you* want to go *there?*" he asks. "The market is not — umm, how shall I say — it is not very clean."

I have to smile. Calcutta is anything and everything but clean. Built atop a swamp the Mogul emperor Aurangzeb gladly rented to the English in the seventeenth century, it may be the dirtiest metropolis on earth. Several feet of backfill have not been enough to bury all the muck on which Britain floated its empire.

The 1981 census lists the city population at nine million, but an official at the West Bengal Welfare Department laughs at that figure, considering it absurdly low. For every person living in a building, at least two people live on the streets. If he's right, Calcutta qualifies as the most populous city in the world.

The official finishes jotting down information from my passport and resumes his warning. "What I meant to say is that the fowl market is not a safe place. I cannot recommend it."

I say nothing, which makes him nervous and even more suspicious. As I soon learn, people sitting behind state desks interpret reticence as disagreement.

"You must answer me. Why do you want to go to the fowl

market?" he says loudly, glancing about the room to make sure his colleagues are watching. If I'm arrested, he wants the others to know that he tried to discourage me.

"I'm looking for the pink-headed duck, Sir . . . a very rare bird."

He scribbles something and begins tapping his head with the pencil. "Who? Do you have an address?"

I explain that the pink-headed duck has no address, at least not a permanent one. Though a half dozen or so appeared each year in the Calcutta fowl market when Victoria ruled as empress, the bird hasn't been sighted for fifty years. And Calcutta, hub of the raj, once the center of the pink duck trade, is the logical place to begin my search. I hope I'll find an old-timer in the fowl market who is familiar with the duck and can point me in the right direction.

The official covers his face with his meaty hands, muttering something I can't understand. I imagine him imploring Vishnu, the Hindu god of preservation, for protection. To calm him I pull out a 1979 edition of Salim Ali's *The Book of Indian Birds.* The author is well known throughout India, and the book is published by the Bombay Natural History Society, keeper of all records concerning the pink-headed duck. I try to pass it to him, but he jerks his hand away and purses his lips. On page nineteen is a color illustration of the duck. Pointing to it, I explain that the pink-headed duck is one of India's greatest treasures, a spectacularly plumed bird, and the rarest, most elusive duck in the world. This intrigues him, and he scrutinizes the plate. The bird's Hindi name is *gūlāb-sīr,* but ornithologists refer to it as *Rhodonessa caryophyllacea.* The last confirmed sighting was in 1935 by a sportsman hunting in the Darbhanga area of Bihar. Unfortunately, he recognized the prize only after wresting it from the mouth of his retriever. Every attempt to breed the duck in captivity failed; in fact, within days of being caged, the birds appeared listless and refused food, defying the intentions of their captors. Without their freedom, pink-headed ducks, it seems, would rather be dead.

I explain that most naturalists believe the pink-headed duck is extinct, but my theory is that it's actually in hiding, having learned, for good reasons, to remain scarce. Although most of its natural habitat around Calcutta has been destroyed, there are still some isolated pockets of undisturbed marshland in the Bengal plain and suitable nesting spots in remote northeast India.

The official remains silent but no longer appears alarmed. I keep up my chatter, hoping that he, too, will appreciate the magic of this beautiful bird. The words tumble from my mouth. At last my fantasy takes shape for him and elicits a laugh.

"You're putting me on, aren't you?"

"No more than I do myself, Sir."

He returns to the map and traces an outline of the game-fowl market, which he refers to now as the easiest place to buy a bird in Calcutta. Handing the map back to me, he grins and says, "At first, I thought you were a drug addict or a smuggler."

"Heaven forbid!"

"Good luck," he says, pushing back his chair and rising. He's taller and fatter than I suspected. He hands me another business card. "Call me if you find it."

With ice a luxury, and refrigeration a symbol of wealth, Calcutta is a city of noxious odors. The fowl market is aptly named: I smell it long before sighting it. I wander along its perimeter, surveying the countless small shops and street vendors hawking birds. Most of the birds are tied at the feet and dangle upside down, suspended from door frames, street posts, or the hands of children; pigeons are cooped ten to a cage; geese, throttled by short lengths of twine, are muted with rubber bands.

I'm uncertain where to begin my search until I spot a parked van and join the queue leading to it. Inside the vehicle an unmuffled generator jiggers loudly; a young man wearing a grease-stained *lungi* is hunched over a copy machine, tweaking knobs and feeding it documents. His two associates lean out a window, conducting business under the sloppy red letters advertising "The Copy Shop."

Hastily I compose a poster of sorts, ripping a color plate from the book and taping the picture of the duck over the caption "LOST! Pink-Headed Duck." In smaller print is the name of my hotel and a request for any information about the bird. The blasting radio and noisy generator render speech useless, so I flash my order for twenty-five copies with my fingers. Acting like an anxious parent looking for a runaway child, I hastily post them around the district.

During my first couple of days in the fowl market, I feel dispirited and out of place. People on the street seem to keep their distance. Perhaps I do look odd: I'm the only westerner walking the area, and because of my height, pale complexion, and baldness, I look a bit like a walking floor lamp, a Gyro Gearloose invention ambling the darker streets of Calcutta.

I develop a routine, awakening before dawn to meet the boats floating down the Hooghly River. Usually they are filled with fresh produce and laborers from the north. I inspect each cargo, hoping to find my duck, constantly showing skippers and crews a picture of the missing bird. By the time the sun slices through the haze coughed up by millions of cook fires, I head away from the river to a teahouse in the center of the fowl market.

Gradually I become more comfortable, and the workers of the district begin to accept me. Inquisitiveness replaces suspicion once they've decided that I'm not a policeman. A cardinal rule of the neighborhood is to avoid the police. "They mean trouble," one vendor informs me, "and who needs more of that?"

On the fourth day everything changes: I'm invited to share a meal, street hawkers start greeting me as the Duck Man, and a few even seek me out before slaughtering their ducks. Soon captains of river boats are inviting me aboard, insisting on taking me for complimentary rides. On a Tuesday I cross the Hooghly sixteen times.

One day toward the end of the week, I finish my waterfront inspections early. The teahouse won't open for another hour, so I walk downstream to a bathing ghat next to the flower market. Nearby, in the shadow of Howrah Bridge, four men stand in water up to their waists. Each is praying in a loud voice while splashing himself.

I strip and dive into the supposedly cleansing water of the Hooghly, a branch of the Ganges and a sacred channel flowing to the home of the gods. For a Hindu, the holiest way to leave this world is to have one's ashes scattered on the Ganges. I swim out toward the middle of the channel, diving for the bottom about fifty yards from shore. As I surface, something bumps the back of my head. Thinking it a stick, I thrust my hand out to fend it off. To my horror, my fingers sink into the spongy remains of a bloated, partially burned corpse. Seconds later my feet are on dry land.

Firewood is scarce in Calcutta because all of it must be transported from the dwindling forests to the north. The price is high everywhere but highest at the funeral ghats. Since the average family in Calcutta earns barely enough to subsist on, the bereaved can seldom afford enough wood to cremate an entire body. When the fires diminish, the remains are simply heaved into the river to be carried out to sea, beyond the beaches of Janput, nearly forty miles away.

Shaken, I rest for several minutes on the stone ramp, staring at my hand. An old man sitting nearby is watching me intently, so I wave and greet him in the traditional fashion, bowing with my hands outstretched, palms together. Ashes are smeared over much of his nearly naked body. He's wearing boxer shorts, and a bell hangs from his neck. Pulling on his beard, he shouts to me: "What did you say? Can't you speak English? Your Bengali is awful . . . Come here and sit by me."

We spend the next several minutes talking about Albany, New York, where he worked as a cook in the early 1960s. He tells me his pigeon pie was famous, the best in the Empire State.

"The governor, that Rockyman, ate my pigeons all the time," he says, picking at his toes.

Upon hearing that Nelson Rockefeller is dead, he muses, "Hmmm . . . must have missed my cooking."

The old man has been watching me for days and wants to know what I'm doing in the district, which he refers to as his "kingdom." I produce the illustration of the pink-headed duck and explain my search. As I talk, he nods in a knowing way, waiting for me to finish before holding out his hand and introducing himself: "Call me Babba, for I am without enemies."

Babba takes the picture of the duck and stares at it for some time. Then he starts to ring the bell around his neck and presses the picture to his forehead.

"Yes," he confides, leaning on my shoulder, ringing the bell louder. "Yes, I know this bird. I know where one lives."

"Let's go!" I exclaim, jumping to my feet. My enthusiasm is not contagious. He motions with his grimy hands for me to sit. Complaining that he's old and infirm, he tells me to calm myself. I continue to beg for directions until finally it occurs to me that money might be able to cure his painful condition. Yes, he will lead me for a price, assuring me that fifty rupees (about four dollars) is the proper balm for his aching body. Babba, friend for life, is able to spot a meal ticket a hundred yards away.

I follow him as he hobbles along the narrow streets. People are selling goods and services of all types. "Sahib need girl? Yank. Yank. Feel good. Suck . . . Ah! Sahib want boy?" But my thoughts are fixated on the pink-headed duck with its cotton-candy feathers and electric-pink bill; not even the alluring smell of opium persuades me to tarry.

The streets deteriorate into alleys awash in green piss as we distance ourselves from the Hooghly and head ever deeper into one of the poorer, tougher parts of town. The decrepit, two-story tenements have dun-colored facades and stockyard odors. Water drips from hand pumps at every other corner. There are no cars and only a few pedal rickshaws, which, like the pedestrians, follow the English tradition of keeping the curb to the left. Groups of men squat near doorways. Whenever I get close, they stop talking and hurriedly fling shawls over items at their feet. Their scowls tell me to keep moving.

"Black market," Babba explains. "Do you need cigarettes? Ivory? Silver?"

Along the curb, rising like giant termite hills, are mounds of trash encircled by human scavengers. Babba explains that recycling is the only legal industry in the area. For the trash pickers, still considered untouchable by many Brahmins, all bits of creation have value, anything can be reborn. Most garbage collection is a family affair, with children stalking the city, returning in the evening to their hovels with burlap bags of discarded treasures. Parents cull the heaps of trash, rearranging them into smaller piles. Cardboard is sold to one broker, tin to another; one buyer even specializes in pull rings from soda cans, paying a penny for every three gross.

"What's the name of this neighborhood?" I ask.

"Heaven's Gate!"

At last my guide stops and waves his arthritic hand toward a small shop. "There, inside that place, you will find your duck," Babba declares as he turns to leave.

I grab his arm and remind him of his promise to show me the pink-headed duck. Steering him back on course, I make a mental note never again to pay in advance for guide services.

Four holy cows, painted with indigo and wearing garlands of marigolds, laze in front of the shop. Flies swarm in tight circles around a row of plucked chickens suspended in the open window. We walk inside slowly, allowing our eyes to adjust to the dimness. The pungent odors of the street mingle with the dank air of the shop. A cleaver lies on a blood-splattered newspaper near the pile of chicken heads oozing at one end of a butcher block. The dirt floor is littered with feathers and entrails.

An obese man emerges from the shadows. With each step, his body shakes, especially his gelatinous face, the color and texture of meat aspic. He talks hurriedly to Babba, far too fast for me to understand. Occasionally he stares at me, running his eyes over my body as if he's sizing up a flank of lamb. I retreat several paces, making sure Babba is between us.

Babba thanks the butcher and moves close to me, saying, "Follow him to the back yard."

"You first."

We walk down a corridor too narrow for the fat man, who has to turn sideways to squeeze through. The light fades with every step, and shortly we're in total blackness. Alarmed, I pull out my flashlight and lag behind, ready to bolt. My apprehension is somewhat dispelled when I hear a muffled but unmistakable *quack.* Ten steps farther on, we enter a shrouded courtyard. Stacks of bamboo cages rise up the walls; most of them are empty, but some contain chickens, none of which are moving. Feathers of all kinds cling to the wooden latticework. An industrial drum full of inky water sits in a corner by the entrance.

The butcher shuffles to the other end of the courtyard and grunts for me to follow. I stay put, shining the beam of my flashlight toward him. So far I've seen no ducks, only chickens.

"The ducks are on the other side," Babba informs me.

I focus the light on a cage the butcher is pointing to. He thrusts his fist inside as if punching someone. A *quack,* loud and clear, draws me nearer. He pulls the bird out, attempting a smile as he speaks.

"He says it's yours for nineteen rupees . . . a good price," Babba interprets.

I close in to identify the duck, steadying the light on its rust-colored bill. What? Yes, a rust bill and a dull brown neck. It's not a pink-headed duck but rather a common red-crested pochard, annual winter visitor to India.

"Please, don't tell him," Babba advises. "Just buy it and we can leave without trouble."

Babba grabs the duck and I hand over the money. Dejected, the two of us leave the shop. Babba doesn't want the pochard; he became a vegetarian long ago. Its wings have been clipped, so we can't release it. I give it to a family living on the street, and we walk back to the river along one of the city's larger avenues. The return trip takes half the time of the original trek down the side streets, but as Babba explains, "You get your money's worth the other way."

At the bathing ghat, I decide to bid Babba farewell. This doesn't sit well with him.

"How can you leave me? How can you be so cruel? Are we not friends? Look at my legs, my hands . . . I will cook for you. Pigeon pie. Duck stew . . ."

"Enough," I shout and lead him into a teahouse.

Over sweet cakes, we agree that he will become my tutor, giving me language lessons for half of every day. He will also act as my guide, with the understanding that when I want to be alone, he will disappear. In return I'll pay him the fifteen dollars a day he has asked for.

This arrangement works well. Occasional problems arise, but Babba is always quick to explain that I'm at fault. My morning routine stays the same, while the time I previously spent prowling the museums and libraries is given over to Hindi lessons. Babba uses the streets as our classroom. We roam Calcutta together, Babba pointing something out and then stating its name in both Hindi and Bengali; a half block away, he tests me on the word or phrase. When I fail, he theatrically asks anyone nearby to help teach me. During the course of a normal afternoon we share pots of tea with four or five different people, all volunteer tutors.

One day, unbeknown to me, Babba tells the workers at the game-fowl market that I will pay a handsome fee for a pink-headed duck. This sends the cogs of local commerce into high gear. A day later, my thirteenth in Calcutta, while standing on the left bank of the Hooghly, I spot one of the riverboat captains sprinting toward me. He's carrying a bamboo cage containing three wildly pink ducks. Fortunately for the birds, the paint is latex and easily washes out.

Only hours later another pink bird is laid at my feet. Fluorescent overspray dapples the sandals of the eager seller, Amrik, a young man who usually peddles screwdrivers and wrenches near the bus stop. What attracts me to Amrik, besides his winning smile, is his capacity for lying. He swears that he has just scooped the bird from the river, insisting that the coloring of all Indian birds comes off when touched by foreigners.

"It's your white skin crying for color," he tells me, gently stroking the bird.

When I point out that he's holding not a duck but a red turtledove, he quickly corrects me: "It may look like a *biki* [Dove] now, but it was a duck."

My eyebrows arch in disbelief; Babba turns away, wheezing, trying unsuccessfully to swallow his laughter. Amrik is undeterred. "It is true," he continues. "You see, when a pink duck leaves the water, it changes into a biki. If it was raining, it would still be a duck, but it is not raining today. That, my American friend, is why it looks like a biki. Don't you understand?"

For a small price I buy the distressed bird from him. As I sit in the back of the teahouse, swabbing the biki first with kerosene and then with soap and water, I decide to leave Calcutta. Originally I had planned to spend only five or six days in this city, and now I can foresee what will happen to me after Amrik brags of his sale, telling his pals that the American will buy any pink bird.

At first Babba is angered by this news, but noting my reaction, he starts chastising himself for being inadequate. "I know why you leave. Because I am miserable, I make you miserable. Because I am poor, I make you feel poor. Because my bones ache, you suffer . . . Yes, you must go. Who wants to watch me die?"

He drones on and on as I try to think of a satisfactory way to part. I summon the owner of the tea shop, and after twenty minutes of haggling, we stand and shake hands. I've just leased the shop for the night in Babba's name. Like the mythical phoenix, Babba rises from the ashes of misery, becoming a new man. He will be the host of a party.

"There is much to do and little time," he says, excusing himself from the table. "I must invite everyone and keep an eye on the kitchen."

I leave for my hotel as Babba begins to harangue the shop attendants, ordering them to clean the place. It's a thirty-minute walk to the Rest Happy Lodge, my residence for the past week. I chose it for its name, cheap price (six dollars a night), and pleasant staff. It's the perfect antidote to the Fairlawn Hotel, where I spent my first nights in the company of impolite westerners, burly Australians, and Japanese shutter-clickers. Where the Fairlawn aspires to recreate the atmosphere of the raj (the employees dress in silly get-ups and call the guests Sahib or Memsab), the Rest Happy, not listed in any brochure, doesn't pretend to be more than it is: a quiet place run by a sleepy family.

Packing is no great chore for me; I'm content to wear the same outfit for days on end. If I need something new or fresh, I buy it. But when it comes to camping and camera supplies, experience has taught me to arrive in a foreign country fully equipped. My gear fills two bags and weighs nearly fifteen kilos. Cameras and film account for most of the weight, and the remainder is survival or medical equipment. I've also brought a variety of presents to give away at opportune moments: a gross of "New York, New York" pencils, a dozen wrist watches with built-in AM radios, plenty of 3-D pins of

Godzilla, and a hundred disposable lighters printed with the image of Michael Jackson.

Two hours later there's a sharp knock at my door. Babba has sent some of his friends to escort me to the party. What a pleasant surprise, I think, until one of them tells me to hurry: the dining and music can't start until I arrive. Music? . . . I didn't hire musicians.

The teahouse is packed; the entire neighborhood seems to be here. Babba is king tonight, and he breaks away from his court to greet me. To my relief he reports that the musicians and the special items he has added to the menu cost less than twenty dollars.

"What's a party without music, Searcher of the Duck?" he asks.

All along I've assumed Babba to be celibate, a man dedicating the last part of his life to god. But as the night rolls on, his true self is revealed. Instead of walking, he starts sashaying; his hands rove and his skinny legs straddle anything warm and round. When I ask him about this, he stands on a chair to shout, "I love sex."

Luckily, only three people bring painted birds to the party. Without much argument, they agree to clean off the birds before joining the festivities. Although many Hindus are disdainful of liquor and drugs, this crowd, the citizens of the fowl market, swig from flasks and light pipes filled with various substances. Off in a corner, near the musicians, people dance, using their eyes and hands to interpret the lively ragas. The party is a success and continues, I'm sure, long after I've left. A little after midnight, as I make my exit, Babba stops the music to make a toast. His words follow me all the way to the hotel.

"To the gods, to us, to the pink-headed duck!"

The next morning Babba is waiting for me in the street. He looks a mess. He hasn't slept, and after all the dancing, his legs really do ache. I hire a rickshaw, and the two of us take a farewell tour of Calcutta. It's mid-September, hot and humid.

Heat radiates from the macadam, making the buildings appear to undulate in the liquid air. There's no wind, and the diesel exhaust from the traffic is suffocating. My urge to revisit tourist attractions wanes with every drop of sweat coursing down the rickshaw puller's back. Babba insists that I'm a fool for worrying about the driver.

"This is his job. You paid a fair price and you should not feel bad."

These words fail to change my feelings. Near the Maidan, a city park, the so-called lungs of Calcutta, I hop out, instructing the driver to take Babba wherever he wishes. My friend leaves his seat to embrace me. We say nothing, knowing that this is good-bye.

One place in the park beckons to me, a small plot of land I call the "Rat Palace." When I first happened upon it, I was shocked, but now, after several visits, I've come to appreciate it. Protected by a low fence of welded hoops, thousands of brown, black, and gray rats lord over one of the few green patches in the city. Their kingdom is a labyrinth of holes and tunnels spread over a quarter acre. Invariably there's a crowd watching the rats race about, tossing them food and cooing, as if admiring a newborn child.

Hindu gods assume many forms in their various reincarnations. Shiva, god of destruction and re-creation, once lived on earth as a rat and, as a result, hundreds of thousands of Indians revere them. The Rat Palace is a living example of Indian adherence to the laws of Karma. Who knows whether that rat is your grandfather?

"Quite a sight, eh?" I suggest to a well-dressed businessman standing beside me.

"It must be strange for an . . . American?"

"Yes, American."

"Calcutta must be very different from your home," he says, aiming shelled peanuts at a massive brown rat. "Where are you from in the States?"

"New York."

"Yes, this is far from New York. Here I am feeding rats on my lunch break. But you know, when I went to university in London, I often went to the zoo to feed the animals. The English love to feed squirrels."

"But these are rats."

"Yes," he says, pausing a moment to study a peanut before tossing it. "But so what? Let me ask you something. Are rats bad? Do they not have a life? . . . Are they lacking status among other animals?"

"Well . . ."

"You don't have to answer. I'm not a Jain, but I do believe all things must be given a chance to live, and we must oblige that law. The poor in this life may become the rich in future lives."

"That is a philosophy I don't understand."

"No, that would be hard for an American."

"A skeptic, please."

"Or a skeptic. Let me give you a better example. I have a friend who owns a flour mill. Twenty percent of his stores were being lost to rats each year. Not long ago he put two cats in the warehouse. That was his solution and, I may add, a very sane one."

"What happened?"

"Oh, now he has many cats and still loses twenty percent to rats. Life continues the same, even though we come and go. And speaking of going, I must return to my office. Will you finish feeding the rats for me? . . . Thanks so much."

I stroll down the path after him, munching the peanuts.

2

Red Tape in New Delhi

"THINK OF ROME and Washington rolled into one and you have New Delhi," reads the first line of a slick travel brochure aboard the plane I'm taking to the capital. Dismayed by the thought of such a blend, I doze off until we're circling above Indira Gandhi Airport.

Through the porthole I can see far below the lights of New Delhi strung out in a vast, precise grid; the streets run in straight lines, true as an architect's ruler, unlike the streets of Calcutta, a city that looks as if it was laid out aboard a yawing man-of-war.

At the airport information desk I peruse the list of government-approved hotels in level three (beyond cheap) and spot the Long Rest and Happy Hotel. I decide to head there; perhaps it's operated by relatives of my congenial hosts in Calcutta. I wander about the airport for a while to let the horde of cabbies and bag carriers expend their energies on the other passengers. When at last I exit, a mob surrounds me. Dozens of hands grab for my bags; cabbies bark exorbitant fares; guides shout conflicting directions. I nod to one driver, who clears a path to his car.

"What was that all about?"

"Bad timing. You were everyone's last chance. The next plane arrives tomorrow morning."

The Long Rest and Happy Hotel, or simply L.R.H., as the

night manager refers to it, is pricier and less appealing than I expected. "We are upgrading ourselves," the manager says, pointing to several buckets of mauve paint near the door. He leads me to an antiseptically clean room.

"Just like America, no?" he says proudly.

"Just like America, yes," I reply, nodding. The room will do until I find something better.

I spend my first day riding city buses, the number six, then the number twenty, and so on for seven hours of circles and transverse lines, never sure where we are going or when I will get off. The bus system is an ideal introduction to the city. A rolling lesson in demographics, it provides access to the various neighborhoods and the people who inhabit them. Babba's Hindi lessons prove invaluable, especially his tutoring in slang. From one of my fellow riders I discover that the city has no game-fowl market. He also doubts that I will find a pink-headed duck anywhere near Delhi.

In a local bookstore I buy a city map and a relief map of the Indian subcontinent. The relief map is brightly colored to mark political divisions, but two areas are unnamed and untinted. One is a narrow section near the giant rhododendron forest of northeastern Sikkim; the other, triangular in shape, lies in the upper Brahmaputra River Valley, near the conjunction of Burma, China, and India.

Why has the printer erased two chunks of the world? Is this uncharted territory or just a mistake? Research in the library and the National Archives suggests that the white areas are indeed unexplored and uncharted. If any outsiders have investigated these regions, I can't locate a record of their explorations.

At last I know where to head next in my search. Where but in a region unseen by modern man, defined only by imaginary lines of latitude and longitude, would the pink-headed duck be hiding? But how to get there? Both areas have been closed to foreigners since Indian independence in 1947. The officials at the Sikkim and Assam state tourist offices in Delhi tell me that only the federal government can issue permits.

I pore over my maps, including those I've brought from America, for routes that lead into the unknown regions without passing too close to army bases or major government projects. After several hours I find what I'm looking for. I will request permits to travel the length of the Tista and Brahmaputra rivers, the major waterways of Sikkim and Assam. Both rivers, fed by the snows of the Himalayas, drain the uncharted areas; both are distant from the rumblings of tribal or international war; and both offer ideal habitats for the pink-headed duck.

Permits are issued at the office of the Ministry of Home Affairs in Lok Nayak Bhavan, a dreary, block-long, five-story building not far from India Gate. Its windows are blackened, sealed by dirt and decay. Rust stains streak the concrete façade. Public bathrooms are near the entrance, but there's no running water, and a putrid smell fills the air. Police and heavily armed soldiers patrol the grounds.

A line of people snakes its way around the corner of the building. Although the office is open only three hours a day, everyone with a visa problem must come here, and this afternoon it looks like every nationality in the world has a representative on line. Concentrating on lesson eighty-five of *Hindi Is Simple,* I wait for my turn to enter.

Two hours later a tired-looking man sitting behind an unpainted plywood desk passes me an application form. The questions are the basic W's (who? why? where? when?) and leave little space for answers. I fill out the form, hoping whoever reads it has a sense of humor. A clerk takes my completed application and disappears down a hallway. Moments later laughter echoes from the next room. The clerk reappears and tells me to return the next day: the undersecretary wants to see me. I leave elated and confident that I will get my permit.

Instead of heading straight for the hotel, I decide to venture down side streets, and I walk for several hours until, footsore, I stop at a teahouse. I ask questions about the neighborhood of the boy serving me. He's polite but too shy to say more than three or four words at once. However, when I ask him if he knows of a good hotel, he points next door and goes on about how wonderful the place is. I survey the whitewashed stucco building and finally spot a sign no bigger than a grapefruit announcing the Grand Life Hotel. There's no mention of it in my travel brochures, and the state Regulatory Office doesn't list it — two good reasons to check it out. The lobby is clean, the price cheap, and the TV room is filled with all sorts of people. Perfect.

The manager is out, so one of the employees takes me on a tour. I like the rooms and place a deposit on number seven, reserving it for the next few days.

Dinner is a private celebration, with me drinking to my own health and brilliance; I've found an intriguing new residence and I'm sure my permit will be granted tomorrow. Yes, I tell myself, eat and be happy, for in a matter of days dinner will be over a campfire on the trail of the pink-headed duck.

The next morning I check out of my old hotel and carry my bags to the Grand Life. The manager answers my hello with a frown.

"I'd like the key to room seven, please. I made a deposit yesterday."

He stares at me blankly, so I repeat myself in Hindi. His nostrils flare. I try Bengali.

"I understood you the first time," he says. "You must be confused. This is not a tourist hotel. Try the Yatri Newas."

I fish in my pocket for the receipt. At this moment I spot the man who accepted my money trying to slink out of the room.

"That guy! . . . He let me register and took my money. Look, here's my receipt."

The manager flies into a rage, yelling at the employee, who keeps his eyes on the floor.

"I am sorry about this. There has been a mistake and you must leave. Here is your money. Please go," the manager says as he stuffs rupees into my hand.

Indignant, I stand my ground, refusing to leave, slapping the money down on the desk. "I'll call the police," I announce reflexively, surprising even myself.

The word "police" has a pronounced effect: every eye in the TV room turns toward me. Small white packages begin appearing and disappearing, slipping from hand to hand until one person bolts for the exit. The manager is breathing heavily, his hands curled into tight fists. A woman dressed in a bikini races up the stairs shrieking, "Mahout, Mahout . . ." Suddenly I realize this is not a normal hotel. I'm about to apologize and leave quietly, when an athletic-looking man breezes into the lobby. His clothes are finely tailored and his bearing elegant. His hair is combed straight back, flipping just below his silk collar.

"Hell-o," he says in a refined English accent. "Welcome to the Grand Life Hotel. Is there a problem?"

The manager speaks too quickly for me to understand everything, but what I do comprehend is insulting. As he finishes, I announce my departure. They can keep the deposit.

"No, wait! You must stay if you wish to," the elegant man says to me. "I am Mahout. What's your name?"

We talk for several minutes, and Mahout's graciousness makes me relax. People slowly return to the TV room, and the manager hands me the key to room seven. Mahout takes the key from me and returns it to the manager.

"Give him room thirteen," he commands, and then says softly to me, "Thirteen is a lucky number in India. I am sure you will like it."

Escorting me up the marble stairway, Mahout pauses on the first step to look me in the eye. "As you can guess, the police are not welcome visitors at the Grand Life. I think you can understand . . . Good. How about dining with me tonight, say around eight?"

Room thirteen is bigger than my entire apartment in New York. Four windows overlook the street where a group of children play cricket. Butted against a pale yellow wall is the largest bed I've ever seen. Off in a corner, under one of the eleven mirrors in the room, sits a long writing desk. Twenty-nine steps from the door is the bathroom, with twin sinks, tub, and shower. I climb into the shower after hanging my jacket close to the billowing steam, hoping some of the wrinkles will disappear.

Later that afternoon I find the line at Lok Nayak Bhavan longer than the day before, but it seems to be moving faster. Attitude, I tell myself, it's all a matter of attitude.

I enter the undersecretary's office with my hand extended, confident in myself and my purpose. The seated official doesn't even look up from his papers. I clasp the back of a chair and introduce myself.

"So you are the man looking for the duck," he says, removing his reading glasses to eye me. "Did you make an application for travel permits through our consulate in New York?"

"Yes, but this one is different," I say.

Months ago, while applying for my entry visa, I had filled out a similar but shorter form. I never received a reply, and several officials at the consulate told me not to worry, that applications often get lost in transit.

"I have your original application in front of me. You request unrestricted travel . . . Pan-India, you say."

"That's true, Sir, but that was before I knew where to look for the pink-headed duck. This new application is only for the Tista and Brahmaputra rivers."

"Which of these applications do you want me to consider?" the undersecretary asks, putting his glasses back on.

"Well, Sir, of course I'd like permission to travel every-where."

"I can answer that right now. No."

The official opens a drawer and pulls out a black plastic comb, which he runs through his hair several times.

"Well? What else?" he says impatiently, putting the comb back in the drawer.

"How about the rivers? Can I follow them?"

"The Tista is off limits. Northern Sikkim is a military zone. Sorry."

"All of the river is off limits?"

"For you and other westerners, yes."

I know that northern Sikkim is a frontier post for eighty thousand Indian troops, one soldier for every four residents of that tiny mountain state. The army is massed along the border with Tibet to prevent a repeat of the Chinese invasion of 1962, when Mao's Red Army stormed into India. But the giant rhododendron forest and the branch of the Tista leading to it are far from any military installation, a fact I mention to the undersecretary.

"That is interesting . . . Tourists don't usually know such things," he says.

"I've done some research."

"My answer is still the same. No," he says, returning to his paperwork.

"One last question, if I may," I entreat. "What about the Brahmaputra?"

"Hmm, I doubt it, but I will have to check before telling you no. Come back tomorrow. That is all . . . Good-bye."

That evening, when I visit Mahout in his elaborate suite, my somber mood brightens. He had told me that he enjoyed the finer things in life, and his apartment is testimony to that. If he likes something, he buys it, no matter how it may challenge the rest of the decor. Fine Persian miniatures hang next to large Dutch paintings in gilt frames; antique statuary sits atop banks of audio and video equipment; two contemporary chairs are lost behind a thick oak table that Henry VIII might have used.

"I am in the import-export trade," he says. "I travel a lot . . . The gods have been kind to me in this life."

While we eat and drink, we trade stories about our lives. As a boy he answered to the name Arun, and he lived a privileged life as the son of a wealthy merchant in Madras. "Then I went to Cambridge and was nicknamed Mahout when I climbed over a fence at the zoo and rode an elephant as a prank."

With dessert we have champagne, and by the end of the second bottle our friendship is sealed. He confides that he's more than just an importer-exporter, adding the title "gentleman outlaw" to his résumé. This, I'm told, means that he shuns violence, guns, heroin, and anything involving children.

"I support many good causes," he says defensively. "I've met Mother Teresa."

Next morning the sky is bright and clear, save the lone black cloud hovering over the Home Ministry. I arrive there an hour early and find myself near the front of the line. The undersecretary greets me cordially before turning me over to a clerk. "Follow him," he orders. "Someone wants to meet you."

We walk down a long hallway with mustard-colored walls and pea-green floors to a small office where two men wearing shiny suits await me. They offer me a cigarette and tell me to sit down. The taller of the two explains that the tape recorder on the desk will help him remember our conversation.

"Welcome to India," the other man says. He is short and skinny and keeps at least one cigarette going at all times. "Would you please tell us about this duck?"

I explain. They stare at me or blow smoke rings. An unnerving silence punctuates the end of my report. Finally the short man shakes his head and says, "This is hard to believe."

It takes me almost forty minutes to convince them that I'm harmless, that my knowledge of army bases comes from research at newspaper offices. At last the tall man looks me straight in the eye and says, "You really are looking for this red duck, huh?"

"Pink."

"Whatever . . . Sounds crazy. What will you do if you find this duck?"

"I'm not sure. I want to learn its song and . . ."

He cuts me off and sends me back to the undersecretary, who tells me to return tomorrow.

Every day for the next week I dutifully appear at his office for news about my application, which I've revised for travel only on the Brahmaputra. I become acquainted with the guards and clerks at the Home Ministry. If I buy the tea, they let me share in their gossip and join their card games during lunch break. Talk usually centers on their work, families, and favorite TV programs. They're fascinated by American stars. "What's Kojak like? . . . How big is Hoss? . . . Is your president still acting? . . ."

Many people advise me to offer bribes to the undersecretary. Mahout claims that baksheesh — what he calls "tokens of gratitude" — is the grease of Indian commerce. The notion repels me. In all of my traveling, I've never paid a bribe and have no intention of starting now. This is a matter not only of principle but of fear. I'm certain I'd be caught. Mahout laughs, but my resolve is final. I'll stick to buying pots of tea and paying for the odd lunch.

On my tenth day in Delhi the undersecretary smiles as I enter his office. He grabs my hand in an especially warm manner.

"I have an answer for you," he says cheerfully. I'm ready to start packing for the trip. I wonder where I should invite him to lunch.

"Unfortunately, your request has been denied. You can't go down the Brahmaputra," he says. I plop into a chair. "Ah, this is so good. I mean that you are not yelling or angry. So many foreigners shout at me when I tell them no . . ."

"Will you change your mind if I start yelling?" I ask.

"Oh, please don't. I hate it when they scream. Here is what you can do . . ." He recommends that I appeal the ruling and promises his help. He considers himself a generous man and makes a phone call on my behalf.

"The director will see you tomorrow . . . Don't forget me. Come visit — I have gotten used to you."

The Indian civil service is modeled on the English system. During the 150 years of the raj the English employed Indians as their administrative assistants and secretaries, the majordomos of Mother England. The empire founded schools and colleges to educate Indians for the civil service, sending many to graduate programs in Britain and providing opportunities for advancement based on tenure and merit, not caste. After independence, this tradition continued, so the bureaucracy is run by the same well-trained men and women no matter which party is in office.

The next day I finally meet the director, a man just two steps below the top rank in the service. At the moment, while his boss is on leave studying at Oxford, he's in charge of all foreigners' requests. Although he's the official who denied my application, I find it impossible not to like him. We both chain-smoke and love chocolate. During the next two weeks I visit him every day, hoping for news about my appeal to the Review Board. We develop a friendship and usually spend an hour shooting the breeze, talking about newspaper headlines, sports, and his favorite topic, education in India.

Mahout is incredulous. "How can you spend so many hours with those boring people?"

I correct him, explaining that they're not boring and that visiting the Home Ministry has become my job. No bureaucrat wants to help a self-righteous foreigner. Why should they? Patience is the key, I tell him; anyone petitioning the government must meet civility with untiring civility. I'm determined to find the pink-headed duck, and if that means spending a couple of weeks making small talk with bureaucrats, I won't complain.

"It could take years! Lay out some cash," Mahout trumpets.

"I'll take my chances playing it straight."

"You're in India; do like Indians."

"No, I'm an American in India, and I'd blow it."

"You will come around. Want to bet?"

"No bet."

Sixteen days after receiving my application for an appeal, the Review Board agrees to consider my case. The director cautions that the verdict is at least a month away; also he doubts they will overturn his decision.

"In India it takes just as long to be rejected as accepted," he tells me.

"I'll make a good impression during the interview."

"What interview?"

"Don't they want to talk to me?"

"No, that is not how it's done . . . Take a break. Leave the capital for a while. Travel. Isn't there someplace you want to visit?"

"Sikkim," I reply without hesitation.

"Ah, they say Sikkim is beautiful, but there are restrictions. Hold on . . ." He flips through a dog-eared directory to check on travel regulations to the Himalayan state and offers me a special fifteen-day pass.

"This is the best I can do for you," he says, stamping my passport with blue and red seals. Next to each he writes something in ballpoint.

"What's that for?" I ask, pointing to his handwritten notes.

"There are only three towns you can visit: Gangtok, Rumtek, and Phodong. The rest of Sikkim is off limits."

That night Mahout and I study the maps and discuss travel strategies. Two "colleagues" he has invited over describe the mountain areas they knew in their younger days as smugglers. Neither of them has a suggestion for reaching the uncharted tract in the far north.

"We only know the south. Nobody goes up there. There are no roads, no towns."

"That's why I want to go."

"For a duck?"

"A pink duck."

After we've polished off a bottle of Sikkimese Bagpiper scotch, Mahout offers professional advice: "Just go to Gangtok and figure things out from there."

3

The Best Driver in All of Sikkim

FROM THE AIR Sikkim looks like an enormous amphitheater hewn out of rock, bounded on three sides by the Himalayas. The main ridge lies to the north, and two spurs jut southward, sealing the former kingdom between Nepal, Bhutan, and Tibet. Only seventy miles long and forty wide, Sikkim boasts more than a thousand different species of orchid growing within its borders. No other place its size has such varied terrain, ranging from dense jungle to glacial plain. The rare snow leopard, the Himalayan black bear, and perhaps the yeti, as well as the pink-headed duck, are all part of its menagerie.

The British, always seeking to define the foreign in their own terms, called Sikkim the "Switzerland of Asia." The original inhabitants, the Lepchas, named their majestic land "Nye-mae-el," or heaven; like heaven, Sikkim is not an easy place to reach.

The plane from New Delhi flies over the state, but it lands about thirty miles below the border on the West Bengal plain. From the airport at Bagdogra, I take an auto-rickshaw to nearby Siliguri, the embarkation point for all buses to Sikkim. I arrive at the depot just in time to watch the last coach of the day to Gangtok disappear over the horizon.

Before 1955 Siliguri was best known for its frightening rates of malaria and infant mortality. Then oil was discovered in Assam, and the mineral wealth of the other northeastern states was uncovered. Because of its geographic position at the western end of the Northeast Corridor (a narrow bridge of Indian land running between Bhutan and Bangladesh, connecting Assam, Nagaland, and the five other northeastern states with the remainder of India), Siliguri became the region's shipping and trucking center. Here the area's major roadways converge, and the railroad track switches from broad gauge to the old narrow gauge installed by the British. The town expanded at a staggering pace and became a city. From the look of things, no one hired a planner or designer. Cinderblock is the height of architectural achievement. What is impressive is the number of gas stations lining the roads, scores of them, stretching for miles.

After visiting a few downtown hotels, I decide to sleep under the stars. The rooms aren't expensive, but I'm concerned about what might be breeding in the closets. I eat dinner at a small restaurant, scooping my rice, dal, and vegetables with my fingers in the traditional manner. I try to ignore the man in the dapper polyester outfit who has seated himself at my table.

"You need a fork!" he says, signaling to a young waiter.

"I'm fine," I tell him. "Don't bother."

"How can you be happy eating like a Kurd? I am educated and I know about diseases. Did you wash your hands?"

"Yes," I lie. For a moment I see my mother in a pew of St. Jude's asking God, "Is he washing his hands and brushing his teeth?"

"All foreigners need help in India, and I am the man for you. My name is Krishna, but please call me Chris."

I decline his offer, pay the check, and pick up my bags. Chris doesn't take the hint and tries to help. I shake my head, but he grabs a bag anyway. I catch his hand and say, "No thanks."

He persists and I snarl, "Chow!" a slang word meaning, when said in anger, "Scram! Beat it, lowlife."

The restaurant falls silent. I've gone too far, publicly embarrassing the man. Even if he's a hustler, he has shown only friendly concern for me. I apologize loudly in Hindi, explaining that I'm tired and need sleep. Four other men dart into the street to summon a rickshaw.

"Hotel Sinclair," Chris instructs the driver, "where all white people stay."

No doubt he receives a commission for sending me to the fanciest hotel in the district. The rickshaw ride to the hotel takes twice as long as it would have taken me (if I had been polite) to send him off in search of other prey, and the room costs me thirty times the price of a drink and dinner. It's an expensive lesson in manners.

At dawn I hurry to the Sikkim bus depot, expecting to secure a seat, but the yard is already jammed with people.

"Is it always this crowded?" I ask another passenger.

"Maybe," he says, flashing lots of gum and one tooth.

"What do you mean, grandfather?"

"When I was young, there was nothing that made me feel crowded. Now that I am old, I see crowds everywhere. For you it should be easy, eh?"

"Right," I say, gathering my pluck for the climb up the back of the bus to the roof. There's a ladder, but the bottom rungs are missing.

"Step on the bumper, then the door hinge, and I will help you from there," calls a voice from the roof. I follow the instructions and join about twenty people already clinging to the rooftop. The bus driver saunters down the path, stopping dead in his tracks when he sees me.

"Hey, what are you doing up there?" he yells.

"Going to Gangtok."

"Have you ever been on this bus before?"

"No."

"Get down! . . . What are you trying to do? If you fall, I lose my license . . . Get down! You can sit next to me."

He thrusts his chin forward as we pull out of the depot,

pedal to the floor. Seeing the look on my face, he tells me not to worry. "I am Ram, the best driver in all of Sikkim."

"I hope so," I reply, watching the scenery zoom by.

"I am going to win the road race next week!" (The Himalayan Rally, that is, one of the most treacherous motoring events in the world.)

Gunning the packed bus along the one-and-a-half lane road, he preens himself in the mirror as I fumble for the nonexistent seat belt. The speedometer is not broken, I'm told, it's just missing the needle. "It's around here someplace . . ."

The view whirling by is of gray, exhausted land, flat to the horizon. Occasionally we pass a cluster of mud buildings with groups of people squatting in front of them, their faces mirroring the barrenness of the landscape. We loop northward, and miles away we see the jagged profile of the Himalayas. Beyond the foothills, close to the top of the world, are Darjeeling and Sikkim.

About sixty-five million years ago most of the world's land masses had assumed the shapes we know today. One exception was India, which was slow to separate from Antarctica. After twenty million years as an island, India rammed into Tibet. The collision folded huge land masses upward and created the Himalayas, which continue to grow approximately two inches every year.

Several miles south of Kalimpong, once the terminus of an ancient trade route between India and China, the bus enters an evergreen forest, and in a grumbling low gear, we start to climb. The steep road, with its many switchbacks and potholes, gives Ram an opportunity to display his driving skills.

We wind through an undergrowth of ferns and moss thriving in the shade of giant sal, teak, and pine trees. Ram tells me that moss is his favorite plant. "I love it. It reminds me of green pubic hair on a woman's mound." The thought inspires him, and he begins telling me about all the women in his life, real and imaginary. As he prattles on, my attention drifts back to the landscape.

For the next fifty kilometers, the road follows the Tista River. Before emptying into the Brahmaputra below Kurigram in Bangladesh, the Tista plummets over 19,000 feet. As the river descends from the stars to the plains, it thunders. According to legend, the sound is the River Spirit singing to Mount Kanchenjunga, the supreme deity of Sikkim. No one has ever paddled the length of the Tista, and as I stare at its foaming rapids, I understand why. Somehow I must find a way to reach one of its tributaries in the north.

At the border separating West Bengal from Sikkim, the bus stops for inspection, and Ram whispers, "Hope your papers are in order. It will be five hours before I return this way."

One of the border guards shouts, "Foreigner! Foreigner!" rousing his colleagues from their cots. Mahout, the hotelier, had advised me to observe the border guards carefully. "If you break the law, they will be the ones after you, not the army. Watch them. Note how they dress, the shine on their shoes . . . Are they well disciplined?"

The bus empties, and everyone else heads to the wall with "Toilet" stenciled on it. I hand my passport to a guard and walk around the compound, looking at the jeeps and trucks. "If the tires are as bald as you," Mahout advised, "it is a good sign. It means the commandant sold the originals to a local dealer. You can make a deal with a man like that." Unfortunately, the tires at this checkpoint have plenty of tread.

Hearing my name called, I walk over to a wooden shack. The two officers inside offer me tea and treat me cordially. The rest of the passengers are already returning to the bus, and Ram is motioning for me to hurry. He starts the bus, revving the engine loudly.

"Is there any problem with my pass?" I ask, declining the tea.

"No, nothing is wrong. One question and then you can leave: Why are you visiting Sikkim?"

"Tourism," I reply.

"Are you an agent?"

"Excuse me?"

"An agent . . . you know, someone buying gems to sell someplace else."

"Oh," I sigh in relief. "Absolutely not."

"Enjoy yourself . . . Remember, it is illegal to buy rubies without state approval."

"Thanks for the warning."

Ram tries to make up for the lost time, shifting gears like a race-car driver. His fastest time from Siliguri to Gangtok was four and a half hours, his slowest was nine days.

"I have never seen the ocean, but on that trip I saw enough rain to fill it."

During the wet season, June to mid-September, the monsoon rains can wash away entire sections of the highway, closing Sikkim to the outside world. The higher we go, the slower we travel, encountering more and more washouts. Frequently Ram must bring the bus to a crawl to navigate rock debris. Even in October the roadway is little more than a dirt path running between giant boulders. Iron plates cap holes big enough to swallow the bus. Ram pays special attention to each plate. "You have to watch them. Sometimes they vibrate and move away from the edge. One scared me yesterday."

Because the road is the main supply route for the frontier army, thousands of workers are employed year-round to maintain it. Most of them come from Calcutta, expecting good pay and housing; unfortunately, it appears that they receive little of either. Every few miles we pass a small shantytown of cardboard hovels erected by a road crew. Their fires are fueled by bamboo and chunks of macadam, spewing thick smoke that covers everything with a black film. Anyone over the age of seven is put to work, and I often find myself watching three generations of one family laboring side by side. Ram declares that the army is the culprit, that it is ruining the roads and the forests.

"Before the army came, there were fewer problems, fewer landslides. But they had to improve the roads. The fools! Instead of pruning, they took out chainsaws. We told them what would happen, but did they listen to us? No!"

Ram tells me he loves nature and hikes all the time. I suggest that the two of us go on a trek. Starting right above the tree line at 16,000 feet, we could descend through all five climate zones on our way to the jungle at the bottom of a deep ravine. Ram pauses and then agrees, with one stipulation: "OK, but only if a car is waiting to drive us back up to a bar."

We pass a road marker with the numeral 4 on it, meaning either kilometers or miles. "I'm never sure," Ram tells me. "We are still a little confused by all this metric stuff."

Whatever the case, in a couple of minutes the outline of Gangtok emerges, its white buildings and cobalt-blue rooftops shimmering in the light.

Gangtok, the capital and only city in Sikkim, is built on the northwest flank of a mountain ridge. It has a spectacular view of Mount Kanchenjunga, the third highest mountain in the world. To the original settlers of Gangtok, animist tribesmen, all of nature was inhabited by various spiritual entities. They chose this spot because every hut could have an unobstructed view of Kanchenjunga, the most powerful of all gods. At dawn the villagers could share the glory of the mountain and watch as the deity crowned itself in golden light.

As the bus slows on the outskirts of the city, the other passengers become lively, talking loudly, squeezing up and down the aisle. I ask Ram for his advice on hotels, and he recommends the Green Hotel: "Good food. I eat there twice a week."

Traffic comes to a halt as a convoy of army trucks passes through. My romantic notion of Gangtok as a sleepy mountain outpost is dispelled with one look out the window. Less than a block away, a giant banner spans the road: "Welcome. Sikkim Fall Festival," it proclaims in English. On a corner a group of teens sways around a boom box, snapping their fingers.

Most of them wear black leather jackets and tight jeans. They spot me and turn up the volume; Mick Jagger belts out "Brown Sugar."

The Sikkimese are not the least bit suspicious of Americans; indeed, of all places in India, Sikkim may have the closest ties to the United States. This bond dates from March 20, 1963, when the *Chogyal* (meaning priest-king) married Hope Cook, a young woman from New York he had met at a reception in Darjeeling. It was the perfect Cinderella story, except that it ended in a bitter divorce years later. In her own way, Hope Cook became an American ambassador and cultural attaché. She hosted parties and barbecues; she sponsored the education of local youths at American universities; she imported American clothing, furniture, and Hollywood movies; and no doubt she carried the first Bloomingdale's bag into Sikkim.

The owners of the Green Hotel are one of only a dozen Muslim households in Sikkim. Pictures of the family patriarch, Sabila, line the wall near the front desk. His widow explains each portrait, telling me the rags-to-riches story of her husband, who was exiled from Lhasa by the Chinese and moved to Gangtok in the late 1950s.

"Honest, hard work will make you more like him," she says, "but you must have a full stomach to follow his footsteps . . . I will get you something to eat." Her eldest son, the manager of the hotel, is a jovial, pudgy man, quick to laugh. When his mother disappears behind the kitchen door, he confides that he "hates work and loves sports." He's a devoted soccer fan and the host of this year's Governor's Cup Tournament, the main event of the Fall Festival. Staying on my floor is the team from Goa, the old Portuguese port on India's west coast.

The hotel opens onto Gandhi Avenue, the main thoroughfare of downtown Gangtok, all five blocks of it. Most of the storefronts advertise bars, haberdashers, or "video theaters," small rooms accommodating no more than two dozen people who pay to watch a video of an old movie. At the end of Gandhi Avenue is Lall Market, which seems tiny after the markets of Delhi and Calcutta, but is adequate to serve the needs of this city of 55,000. I locate the game-fowl section, and by my count there are nineteen bird vendors, six with stalls, the rest operating from the street. Oblong bamboo cages are stacked in front of each seller. Because ducks fetch a high price, they are usually brought to market rather than eaten by their captors. Also, because the market is the center for town gossip, people here will know if an unusual bird has been sighted in the wild.

"Ducks? Do you have ducks?" I ask one vendor.

"Tell me what you want and I will get it."

I take out the picture of the pink-headed duck. A crowd gathers as I describe my quest. Mallards, pochards, widgeons, and other common ducks are well known, but not the pink duck.

"I would know," says an elderly man everyone treats with respect. "I am Chamla Lepcha . . . I came to the market in the year of the horse and have seen three more years of the horse." (Four twelve-year cycles.)

"Do you know this duck, grandfather?"

"No . . . It is such a pretty bird."

He promises to pray for me and my mission. No one thinks my search odd or, if they do, they're too polite to mention it. One man, a seller of carrots and cabbages, swears that if he ever finds the duck, he will keep it until I return. A spice trader, an elderly woman leaning on a cane, moves close to me. She studies the illustration for quite some time. "This duck is god's work," she concludes.

Four days later I change hotels to escape the soccer teams and their all-night carousing. I move down the street to the Hotel Tibet, a moderately priced establishment owned by the Dalai Lama. That morning, as I drink my tea and gaze out the window at Mount Kanchenjunga, a man approaches my table.

He's wearing traditional Bhotia robes of fine quality, and he introduces himself as R. P. Lama, a retired farmer and orchid breeder. He has seen me walking around town and offers to take me on a personal tour of the area. He is about to set off on his daily stroll and would enjoy some company.

As we start climbing the terraced city, he points out ten new buildings for every one he remembers from his childhood. Hillsides that once were pastures are now crowded with multi-storied, concrete-slab tenements. He takes me to what used to be his favorite spot, now a lot filled with slag, garbage, and heavy machinery.

"This was a glade. I used to come here to meditate," he says loudly, speaking over the din of a nearby cement mixer. "There were many butterflies, and flowers were everywhere. I felt close to all things when I sat here. Now my heart cries. Look at these ugly buildings. Unneeded . . . unwanted."

We spend most of the morning together and agree to meet every other day to walk about. He promises to teach me about the flora of Sikkim, especially its orchids. R. P. Lama is a representative of the old order, the life of Sikkim before it became part of India in 1975. He was an aristocrat, born into a family with close ties to the Chogyal. When he was a boy, and Sikkim a theocratic, feudal state, he was one of the very few who were able to enjoy its fruits.

After one of our strolls I venture into a video rental store, curious to see what's on the shelves. Most of the cassettes, like the western goods in the market, are smuggled through Nepal. Several hundred titles are available, many of them current American releases. Judging from the posters and advertisements taped to every available surface, including much of the ceiling, John Travolta and Michael Jackson are the most popular stars in Sikkim. A man in the shop watches me browse before introducing himself as Vijendra. We talk for several minutes, and he invites me to dinner. "After we eat, we can watch this," he says proudly, holding up a tape of *Saturday Night Fever*.

Vijendra, the son of a peasant, is a member of Gangtok's emerging middle class. Both he and his wife have college degrees, which are hung in ornate frames in their three-bedroom apartment. They're enthusiastic about the changes in Sikkim, applauding what R. P. Lama condemns.

"I was one of five children who grew up on a dirt floor no bigger than this living room," Vijendra tells me. He goes to the kitchen and turns on the faucets. "Water, running water . . . When I was a boy, I had to carry buckets from the stream."

He knows his apartment building is a plain, uninspired structure, but that matters little to him. "I don't really care as long as it stays up."

"But what about the beauty and views that are being destroyed?" I ask.

"What is one view in Sikkim, a land of a million views? What is one man's memories compared to families without homes? . . . My father never had anything. He was a slave to a king."

The modern history of Sikkim began in the seventeenth century, when three priests of the Gelupka, or "Red Hat" sect of Buddhism fled Tibet during the great schism. Fearing for their lives, and sharing a common vision of a new Buddhist state, they made their way over the mountains into Sikkim, then known as Denzong, or Land of Rice. They eventually formed an alliance with Phunstug Namgyal, leader of the indigenous Lepcha community. He was invested with the title of Chogyal, and with the help of the priests he consolidated his power and began converting the Lepchas to Lamaism. Bhotia tribesmen, loyal to the Red Hats, steadily migrated from Tibet and were accepted by the tolerant, passive Lepchas. In time a feudal state evolved, headed by the Chogyal and administered by the Bhotia lords.

The country flourished for the next two hundred years, but the Sikkimese army, being better dressed than trained, was unable to keep out hostile troops from Nepal, Bhutan, and Tibet, all of which started annexing large tracts of their land. In the mid-nineteenth century the Chogyal asked the British for help; they too, eventually stole hundreds of square miles around Darjeeling and Kalimpong. After repelling the Tibetan invasion of 1888, the British dominated Sikkimese politics, controlling all of its foreign affairs. When Britain relinquished power in India in 1947, the distant bureaucracy in New Delhi assumed the British role.

For the most part, daily life continued into the 1960s much as it had for the previous three centuries. However, one major change occurred in the fabric of the country: Gurkhas, hillsmen of Nepal, were brought in by the English as laborers for construction projects and tea estates. By World War II the Gurkhas had become the largest ethnic group, displacing the alliance of Bhotias and Lepchas. Unlike the Lepchas, the Gurkhas are descendants of a warrior culture.

I try to visit the Chogyal's palace, but the gates are closed to anyone but invited guests, who, I'm told, are few and far between. The present Chogyal, stepson to Hope Cook, has been stripped of power and leads a reclusive life, spending most of his time meditating. I stretch my arm and throw the stone I'm holding over the palace wall. It lands with a click. Thirteen years ago, in 1974–75, rocks were being thrown at the palace by angry Gurkha mobs demanding an end to feudalism. The Chogyal Palden Namgyal, alarmed, and reportedly distracted by his divorce proceedings, naively asked India for troops to protect his rule.

It is generally believed that India bankrolled and advised the opposition to the Chogyal. Because of Sikkim's strategic location as a buffer separating India from Tibet, Nepal, and Bhutan, New Delhi had long coveted it. After the troops arrived, India forced electoral reforms on Sikkim, which culminated in a referendum calling for the merger of Sikkim into the Indian Union. On April 26, 1975, the Constitutional Amendment Act made Sikkim the twenty-second Indian state. Federal money began pouring into Sikkim, and as roads, housing, schools, and hospitals were built, opportunities for graft and corruption blossomed.

Jigme Kazi, the editor of a weekly Gangtok newspaper, tells me things are improving: "We are finding a balance, but you must try to imagine what it was like. We were like children outside a candy store, able to look, but not allowed inside. Finally, when we could go in, we stuffed ourselves."

Sikkim is a major producer of cardamom and also exports large quantities of ginger, tree fruit, and herbs, but its most famous product is liquor.

"That's the reason," one friend jokes, "we call Gangtok the Happy Valley."

The British, impressed by the purity of the water in Sikkim, established several distilleries in the nineteenth century, and the formulas they perfected then are still in use. The cherry brandy made in Rangpo is reputedly the best in Asia. Among the many brands of scotch, brandy, and beer, my favorite is a lager named Hit, which, as the label says, "is a knockout beer, no less than 8.9% alcohol."

While Siliguri has gas stations, Gangtok has bars. It may be the only city in India where saloons outnumber teahouses. Day and night these bars are crowded with government workers, politicians, day laborers, farmers, barbers, shopkeepers, young and old, male and female. After visiting most of the establishments in town, I've become a regular at a bar down the block from the Green Hotel, where I still eat many meals.

On my tenth night in town I finish dinner and walk the hundred paces to my usual seat at the bar. I'm meeting some of my new friends, but I'm early, so I nurse my beer. The music is blaring; I think it's AC/DC trying to imagine life without heavy metal. A white vinyl floor reflects banks of high-watt fluorescent bulbs; wood-grain contact paper covers the tables, accenting the vibrant green Naugahyde chairs. Posters of American pop stars and brightly painted Indian saints compete for attention along the far wall. A statue of Buddha sits atop a cash register, his lacquered hands clutching small bundles of toothpicks.

After my second beer, a man about my age approaches. He wears the robes of a poor farmer, but his sandals and his supple hands speak of another way of life. Introducing himself, he remarks that he saw me several days ago at the opening ceremonies of the Buddhist meditation center, Sa-Ngor Chostog. The Sakya Trizin, leader of the Sakya sect and one of the holiest men in Buddhism, gave the keynote speech to a crowd of several hundred Buddhists, a handful of Hindus, and one foreigner.

"You are a lucky man to have been blessed by His Holiness."

"Honored more than lucky," I say, motioning for him to join me.

His name is Sonam, which, he quickly tells me, means "virtue." His head is shaved as smooth as a crystal ball, his eyebrows have been plucked, and there's no hair on the back of his hands.

"May I ask you two questions?" he inquires, glancing quickly about the room.

"Feel free."

"Can I trust you? . . . That is good. My second question is whether you think the Chinese should leave Tibet and the Dalai Lama be returned to power?"

"Well, I believe the Chinese are there by force. Can I buy you a drink?"

Such direct questioning of a foreigner is not unusual in Sikkim. Usually people just want to practice their English, but sometimes they want to know what an outsider thinks. However, I decide not to mention my negative feelings about the Dalai Lama's theocratic government.

"My question is do you think the Chinese should leave?"

"Yes, they should go tomorrow and let elections decide what happens. What about that drink?"

"No, thank you. I am studying to be a priest . . . I am happy. I knew you were on our side."

"Our side?"

"Yes, our side. Justice. I have prayed at the feet of my master, and with his blessing I now put the course of my life in your hands."

"I wouldn't do that if I were you. You don't even know me."

"But I do know you, and I must trust you."

For the next fifteen minutes I listen politely to Sonam, the rebel priest. He tells me the Chinese are a godless people, bent on enslaving Asia. He lists crime after crime, blaming them all on Beijing. I'm relieved when he finally leaves and I get to join my friends at another table.

"Who was that?" they ask.

"An angry refugee who went on and on about the Chinese. Not very pleasant."

With that, the discussion turns to a trip we've planned for the next day to visit Ganju Lama, Sikkim's favorite son and a famous war hero. We have to leave early in the morning, so I excuse myself after the third round of beer and head back to my hotel.

I open my door, flick on the light switch, and find Sonam sitting at the desk. A Buddhist prayer scarf with a marigold blossom on each corner is folded atop my pillow.

"Gifts from my teacher," he says.

"Thank you," I reply, "but how did you get in. Wasn't the room locked?"

"I think you will be surprised by the powers of Lamaism . . . Can we continue our talk?"

"I must get up at dawn. Maybe tomorrow night."

"You have good cameras. Very expensive ones, yes?"

"What?" I notice that my camera bag is open. Nothing is missing, but I'm upset that he would go through my things. I assess my options: I can order him to leave or I can listen to him some more. "OK, Sonam, you've got ten minutes and then I'm going to bed."

He tells me he was born in Lhasa in 1954. The oldest son of a prosperous merchant, he fulfilled tradition and parental dreams when he entered a monastery at the age of four.

Within a year his meditative life was turned upside down. Violence broke out in Lhasa; Chinese troops patrolled the streets with bayonets drawn. When the Dalai Lama fled to sanctuary in India, it was the beginning of a mass exodus of monks, Sonam among them.

"All I had," he tells me, "was my faith and my promise."

Sonam made his first trip back to Tibet in 1984, celebrating his thirtieth birthday less than a mile from his birthplace. Since then, wearing the disguise of a farmer, he has illegally crossed the border numerous times, smuggling letters and money to brethren in Tibet, and returning to India with sacred texts, statues, and other holy objects which, he says, "Maoists scorn and destroy."

"Look at the time," I moan.

"There is more."

"Tomorrow night," I suggest, walking toward the door. He doesn't move. His black eyes remain fixed on the spot where I was sitting. I open the door and point outside, saying, "I think you should go."

"But you are a journalist. You must want to know more."

"You've got it all wrong," I say curtly. "I was a journalist, but not anymore, not for years. Right now I'm a tired tourist searching for a duck."

"Yes, the pink-headed duck, gūlāb-sīr. My teacher and I know all about your search."

This doesn't surprise me; I've been asking everyone I meet whether they've seen the bird. Feeling that I've been polite long enough, I begin to order him out. He raises his hand and interrupts me.

"The other night my master and I shared a dream about you. Both of us saw you in the water . . . holding on to a boat. There was no land . . . endless sea. A storm and then calm as you neared death."

I close the door and return to face him. "How do you know this?" I ask, startled that he could know of my rescue at sea years ago in the Atlantic, halfway around the globe.

"I know very little," he tells me.

"I don't understand."

"Few people do," he says. "My teacher will help you. He has answers where I have none."

Now I want him to stay and tell me more about his dream. He adds few details but goes on at length to explain that Lamaists regard every dream as a message with particular significance. Dreams aren't considered links between the conscious and subconscious, but rather spiritual images that connect the individual with the whole of the universe. They are navigational lights, so to speak, used to guide the individual beyond himself.

Sonam pauses, his eyes searching my face. He changes tempo, speaking now in a slow but determined cadence. "I have come to ask for your help. We must free Tibet from the Chinese oppressors."

"We?"

"Would you be willing to go to northern Sikkim and then Tibet? I will take you there."

"I'd love to go," I exclaim, "but how?" The entire country of Tibet is off limits to foreigners because of the recent rioting in Lhasa.

"Leave that to me."

"OK, but what's the deal? I mean, can I just travel around, go where I want, and look for the duck?"

"There will be little time for that. Do you have any maps?"

I pull one out, and he points to Gyangze, a Tibetan town about 150 miles from where we sit. "What's there?" I ask as he circles the name.

"Poison. That is where the Chinese poison is. Truckload after truckload of death . . . Radioactive waste."

According to Sonam, the Chinese have been dumping massive amounts of nuclear waste in the Gyangze area for ten years, maybe more. Initially none of the residents took notice of the waste depot; it was just another secretive military project until a group of Lamas came to investigate. Even today, Sonam asserts, the hillsmen near the dump have little knowledge of the effects of radiation.

"They have no idea what TV is," he says.

"Have you seen this place?" I ask. His allegation, if substantiated, would be important news.

"Monks never lie . . . I have not been there, but other monks have."

He assures me that it won't be difficult to approach, saying, "The Chinese believe their secret is safe."

The dump sits at the bottom of a ravine, and we should be able to look down on it undetected from high above. There are guards, but Sonam insists our guides will know where to hide us. His plan calls for a foray into Tibet lasting no more than four days. We will travel at night and shoot the pictures early one morning. If I get a chance to inspect the flora and look for the duck, it will be while concealed behind a rock. The only things I must bring are my cameras and some camping gear.

"Do you want to go?" he asks, rising from his chair.

This proposal is far too intriguing to pass up. We conclude the arrangement with a handshake. As he is about to leave, he tells me not to change hotels; he will contact me soon. When? He slips into the dark hallway without answering.

The next morning I'm awakened by a loud thud. Another knock shakes the door, and the waiter barges in with a tray of tea, announcing, "Your friends are waiting for you in the lobby."

Suddenly remembering the trip to Ganju Lama's house, I jump up, gulp the tea, and ask the waiter to take my hot-water bottle to the kitchen and fill it with triple-strength tea. It's a trusty device I've learned to rely on; a water bottle is more compact than a thermos, and it keeps me warm at night in the coldest weather.

My three friends and I join the owner of a jeep and head westward toward Rumtek, the site of a famous monastery I've already visited. As we near the sacred place, the driver turns to me, asking if I want to stop. I shake my head no. I wasn't impressed by this modern structure built twenty years ago to replace the original, which was destroyed by fire. While pictures of the ancient monastery depict a beautiful example of classical Himalayan religious architecture, the new one lacks grace and detail.

When we leave the Rumtek district, I remind my fellow passengers that we're breaking the law; my travel permit prohibits me from going any farther.

They assure me that there are few policemen outside the city and that the army doesn't meddle in state affairs but concentrates on the frontier. "So who is going to stop you?" M.M. says. "New Delhi makes these rules and nobody here likes them. Go where you want." He adds, "The police know about this trip. They don't care."

M.M. became my friend after I stopped him on the street to ask for directions to the river, and he led me to a bar instead, explaining, "It is best to have two or three Hits before taking a long walk." Like many people I meet in Sikkim, he goes by the initials of his first two names. He tells me that most Nepalese given names are too long and descriptive to use. "In English my names mean Taller Than a Tree and Gentler Than a Deer. Initials are easier, but I must say that the letter carrier has it bad."

Occasionally I ask the driver to stop so I can crawl into a thicket to look for orchids. I want to bring a present back to R. P. Lama, who has spent hours instructing me about the plants of Sikkim. The brilliant, waxy green vegetation grows thicker and lusher as we descend to lower altitudes. My machete is back at the hotel, so I'm able to penetrate the wild tangle for only a few yards, not far enough to capture a prize orchid. At one stop I take a breath and air my pink-headed duck call, a sound M.M. likens "to a yak in pain." Butterflies swarm about me in the dappled light, but alas, no duck, not even a jungle parrot, returns my call.

Four hours after leaving Gangtok, we arrive at the cardamom estate given to Ganju Lama by the Chogyal for his exploits during World War II. Having been awarded the Victoria Cross, England's highest military award, Ganju Lama still receives invitations from the queen to attend court ceremonies and military parades.

In 1944, as a teenage member of the Seventh Gurkha Rifles, he saw action in the Burma campaign. When the Japanese invaded India and threatened to push on to Calcutta, Ganju Lama destroyed five tanks, two of them singlehandedly, near Imphal, the state capital of Manipur. An enemy bullet was lodged in his thigh for twenty years before it surfaced from the bottom of a boil. "Ganju's bullet" now hangs on a plaque inside regiment headquarters.

Major-General J. A. Robertson reported that Ganju's deeds had turned the tide of battle, "saving thousands of lives." Lord Mountbatten pinned the Victoria Cross on him during a ceremony at New Delhi's Red Fort.

"I was a simple soldier," Ganju Lama tells me as I admire the ribbons and medals filling his display case. Now he's trying to live the ideal Buddhist life. "I dedicate every day to performing good works," he tells me. "You see, I am trying to atone for a bloody past." He reaches for his prayer beads and fingers them while leaning toward me and saying, "Would you like to know whether I would do it again, whether I would repeat the bloody past? The answer is yes. As long as I am fighting for freedom, I will fight."

The teachings of Buddha condemn war and violence, and I ask him how he reconciles this with his life as a soldier. "I cannot . . . I am merely human. I made mistakes. Lord Buddha would have found a way to avoid war; he would have brought peace."

We go into an open room, plainly decorated, with straight-backed chairs lining two walls, to eat a lunch of nettle soup, yak stew, tubers, and tapioca pudding. My request for a third dessert embarrasses my friends but endears me to our hostess.

She takes me on a tour of the kitchen, pointing with pride to the wood-burning stove, a massive iron cube with two ovens. Motioning for me to keep quiet, she stuffs my pockets with small pastries.

Before I get a chance to see the rest of the cardamom estate, M.M. announces that it's time to head back. We hop into the jeep and rush to cover as much ground as possible before darkness. When the sun drops behind the mountains, driving becomes increasingly dangerous and the temperature plunges. My admiring remarks about the "simple soldier" lead to a general discussion of Gurkha troops.

"Who are the best fighting soldiers in the world?" M.M. asks, and answers his own question: "Gurkhas! We are the best."

I can't disagree. Their prowess in hand-to-hand combat is legendary. They were the first British troops to land in the Falklands, as well as in Borneo, Congo, and the Suez. Several years ago an English journalist told me that during the Falklands campaign, the Gurkhas sneaked up on the Argentinian army trenches in the middle of the night and slit the throat of every third man along the line. Screams of horror echoed at first light.

"Do you know how many Gurkhas have won V.C.s [Victoria Crosses]?" M.M. asks, and answers himself again, "Twenty-six. That is right. Twenty-six. There is no better fighter in the world. Just look at Darjeeling."

"Darjeeling?" I ask, thinking of tea and resort hotels.

"Right now there is a war going on. Didn't you know that?"

He tells me of the battle raging just across the Sikkimese border, pitting the Gurkha hillsmen against troops from the plains. As in Sikkim, Gurkhas form the majority in the Darjeeling-Kalimpong area of West Bengal. Many of the fighters, M.M. tells me, are retired English army officers, well trained and willing to utilize their skills in the struggle to establish Gurkhaland as a homeland for the millions of Indian Gurkhas.

"We have nothing in common with Calcutta, so why should

they control us? We want our own state in India, a place where we are safe, where we can live and grow in peace."

"Sounds good," I remark.

"This is serious. People are dying . . . fighting for freedom. You should see what I mean, then you would understand. Freedom, it is all about freedom."

He reveals that he's a member of the Gurkha National Liberation Front (GNLF), which is ostensibly a political party. M.M. intimates that it also controls the guerrillas.

"The GNLF is fighting for Gurkhaland. You must see it. Yes, come to Darjeeling."

"Well," I say, pausing to think about Sonam and the trip to Tibet. Sonam had mentioned spending four days across the border; surely it will take us a full day to get to the frontier and another to return. Allowing for problems and weather delays, I calculate it to be a ten-day trip. Afterward I must return to New Delhi to check on my travel permit for the Brahmaputra.

"I'm sorry, but I can't . . . It might be a month before I could go, maybe longer."

"The struggle has been going on for years," he says, slapping me on the back and promising to make the necessary arrangements. "Come when you can. I will take care of it."

The next morning, back at Hotel Tibet, I awake to find Sonam once again sitting at my desk. His eyes are closed, his prayer beads draped over his folded hands. I move quietly to the bathroom, but the glass I carry slips through my hands and splinters around my bare feet.

Sonam rises and hands me my shoes, saying, "Why were you trying to walk like a cat?"

"I thought you were asleep."

"Thank you, but I was aware of every breath you took."

"I thought meditation was an exercise in isolating yourself from your surroundings."

"There are many approaches."

We go into the dining room for breakfast. The waiters, normally efficient and polite, are excessively attentive, hovering around us. A special tea is brewed, followed by a special bread and an assortment of special jams. Everything this morning is special. Why? The waiters point at Sonam, who speaks to them in a clipped voice, saying something in Tibetan that makes them scatter.

He has shown me his Green Book, the so-called passport Tibetans in exile are issued by the Dalai Lama. Each week the bearer presents it to the local council and, for a rupee, the passport is stamped. In the future, when Tibet is free, these books will be proof of allegiance to the Dalai Lama. Usually these books are unadorned and cheaply made, but Sonam's is leather-bound and embossed in gold, bearing many wax seals. He won't tell me what the gold leaf and filigree denote, saying only that his book was made by a friend in Dharmsala.

Sonam ends further questions by placing his watch — no, that's *my* watch — on the table. We are sitting across the table from each other, and I can't remember him touching me. He of course refuses to say how he got it. I ask if he's a *lung-gum-pa,* a monk who shares the secrets of powerful magicians and psychic voyagers, ascetics who purportedly can levitate. Instead of answering, Sonam begins telling me stories about the power of lamas. He dwells on the mountain mystics, the *respas,* who are experts in Tumo, the art of creating heat without fire. One of their most confounding abilities is that of melting a circle of snow up to six feet in diameter, using only body heat. Sonam reveals that the teachers of Tumo enter and leave their bodies at will, as do Bodhivistas (living Buddhas).

"How else can they survive in the mountains with no clothes?" he asks rhetorically. "They are also *dupchens,* so they are never lonely. They send messages on the wind, always talking to the Eternal Stream of Energy."

"Are you a dupchen . . . Can you read my mind?" I ask nervously, wondering if I still have a private thought.

"Your face and eyes tell me all I need to know."

Sonam hands the watch back to me, saying, "Before thirty-six hours go by, we will be on the road to Tibet."

"I'm ready."

"Are you?" he returns. "Do you understand the danger?"

"I know what happens if we're caught: I'll get deported, and you will . . ."

"I know. I will start the next cycle of life."

The morning news begins on the dining room TV. Today's lead story is the rioting in Lhasa. A Chinese soldier has been killed, and the authorities are extracting revenge through mass arrests and indiscriminate beatings. Details are sketchy, coming from expelled tourists and anti-Chinese sources. The room is now packed with Buddhists following the developments in their mother country. The Indian newscaster announces that the border patrols have been increased on both sides.

Sonam turns to me and whispers, "You must trust me."

I leave after breakfast to reserve a seat on the next day's helicopter flight to the Bagdogra airport in West Bengal. With only a day left on my tourist pass, it's important that I officially check out of Sikkim. According to our plan, Sonam will pick me up at the airport late in the afternoon, and from there we will head back into Sikkim under cover of darkness.

After writing thank-you notes, I search out M.M. and find him in a teahouse. He's full of enthusiasm. "Everything is set," he tells me. "You can go to Darjeeling whenever you are ready . . . Send a telegram to this address when you know your plans."

4

On Lama's Business

THE HELICOPTER FLIGHT to the plains takes a mere thirty-five minutes, almost five hours less than the bus. There are only two other passengers, a rotund couple the captain has seated on opposite sides of the British-made chopper. I ease into a plush seat directly behind the cockpit. We lift off, and I watch as the landscape flattens; the mountains recede, giving way to forested hills rolling into the vast alluvial plain.

With hours to pass until my rendezvous with Sonam, I leave the Bagdogra airport and head into downtown Siliguri to browse at the market. Before entering the bazaar, I stop at a teahouse. It's a beautiful day, and not even the filth of Siliguri can get me down. The waiter brings my tea, placing it carefully in front of me. As I take a sip and lean back to savor the taste, the cup catches on a shirt button and the hot tea spills all over my pants. I jump up and step on the tail of a dog, which yelps and bolts from under my table. The dog gets tangled in the waiter's legs, upsetting his trayful of tea cups. I apologize and leave a generous tip, but that doesn't stop him from shouting at me halfway down the block.

Later, as I near the market, the din of the city is pierced by the harpy screech of worn car brakes, metal grinding metal. A dull thud is followed by a moment of grim silence. I join several others running toward the accident. Around the corner a young man is writing in pain, pinned under a rickshaw. A black sedan is angled across the street, its shaken driver still behind the wheel. I push through the crowd to help lift the mangled rickshaw off the victim. The man is bruised and in shock; we comfort him until the police arrive.

After he's in the ambulance, I head on for the market, stopping at a hardware stand. I'm trying to decide which of two screwdrivers to buy when someone shouts, "There he is! The white man." I turn as two policemen confront me.

"Drop it! Drop it," they order, staring at the tool in my hand. My questions, I'm told, will be answered at the police station. A small crowd has gathered, and I hear people cluck, "He's the one . . . Him . . ."

Inside the dilapidated station house, the accused driver slumps with his head in his hands. He has been crying. I face the roomful of police and raise my voice.

"I demand to know the charges. I demand . . ."

"Ah, you speak some Hindi. That is good for you," says a man in a suit. He informs me that there are no charges, I've been brought in as a witness.

"I didn't see the crash, I only heard it," I tell him.

"Please, just fill out this form," he says.

He points to the driver and asks if I've ever seen the man before. I say no. He hands me a pencil and advises me to make myself comfortable, there may be other questions later. I sense that this could take all afternoon.

An hour later three witnesses are brought in from the street. At first, none of them will cooperate, refusing to give their names or addresses. The police respond with threats of jail. Suddenly memories clear and tongues wag — each of them saw the accident. With that, I'm released, and I race to get a cab.

"Airport, as fast as you can go."

Sonam arrives precisely on schedule, driving a 1954 Land Rover. The car looks great and sounds awful. The engine wheezes and coughs black smoke.

"How did it go?" he asks, mistaking third gear for first and stalling out.

"Fine," I answer.

The engine refuses to catch, and Sonam nearly burns out the starter motor. I detect the problem and push in the choke. On the third try, the engine purrs.

"I am not a very good driver," he reveals, forgetting to clutch and stalling again.

"How will we get to Gyangze?"

"I will get better, I promise," he says. "Anyway, we are not going to Gyangze, but to Guru, which is not as far away."

"Guru? Wait a minute, you told me Gyangze is where the Chinese are dumping the nuclear waste."

"They might be, but I know that they are putting it in Guru."

"What?"

"I had to tell you Gyangze," he says, admitting his lack of trust in me. "Relax, my friend, it will be two or three days before we start for the border."

"Why? It's only ten hours to Natu-La Pass." For centuries Natu-La has been the most common entry point for travel into Tibet.

"You are right, but we are not going there. With the situation as it is along the border, we will go by another route . . . The more distance we travel, the more I can tell you."

Sonam has been less than frank with me. My trust in him wanes as he slowly details the latest agenda. We're not leaving for Guru, we're going to his master's retreat for a blessing. We will not be crossing the frontier in the Rover, we will be walking across an unidentified high-altitude pass. My pal Sonam, the sincere lama concealed in the robes of a dirt farmer, is cagey and manipulative. I remember Mahout's advice: "Leave the instant you feel a setup. Always follow your instincts. People get caught because they don't listen to themselves."

"Sonam," I ask, "did you read my mind or did you really have that dream about me in the boat?"

"My master and I shared a dream," he says, meeting my stare and slowing the car.

"And it was because of that dream that you came to me?"

"The truth is the dream. Your presence made me think, but the dream made me act."

I ask whether there are any other surprises. He shakes his head no.

As I have already discovered coming back from Ganju Lama's house, night driving in the mountains is perilous. With Sonam at the wheel, we constantly skirt disaster. At least he drives slowly and follows my advice on gear shifting. As we near the border of Sikkim, Sonam pulls off the road. We rearrange a space in the back for me to hide among the bags of rice and tins of mustard oil. This is where I will ride for the rest of the trip. He adds to my camouflage by pulling two bags of rice on top of me.

"Can you breathe?"

"Barely."

"That is all you need."

We near the border checkpost, and Sonam warns me not to make a sound. He tells the guards that he's delivering food to a monastery in the mountains. We're allowed to pass without inspection, and for the next six hours I drift in and out of sleep. When the engine sputters and we roll to a stop, my heart races.

"What's happening?" I whisper, thinking the police are closing in.

"Petrol. We are out of gas."

I crawl out of the back and stand in the crisp night air, stretching toward Andromeda, which for an instant seems close enough to touch. Lowering my gaze, I see Sonam holding one hand on the gas cap and the other on his prayer beads. Over and over, he chants "Om mani padme houm." I wonder if he thinks his mantra will fill the empty tank. I then check out our surroundings with a flashlight. We are on a dirt road; there are no other lights; the moon has set. The pines and black poplars suggest that we are above 9,000 feet.

"Om mani padme hoummm," moans Sonam.

"Hey, Sonam . . . are we near an army base? Is this road used much?"

He stops praying long enough to say, "The road has many paths and devils are everywhere."

I pester him again, and he finally pockets his beads to address our predicament. Sonam estimates that we're four or five miles from the house of his master. The nearest army base is far from here, but this byway services it, and we must be cautious. If a vehicle comes along or anyone approaches on foot, I will hide in the brambles while Sonam deals with them. We walk on opposite sides of the road, talking in low voices. His performance back at the car has raised a very important question. If we encounter a Chinese patrol in Tibet, will he reach for his beads or run with me?

"I will be ahead of you," he announces in an imperious voice. Apparently devils like those who tinkered with the gas tank will not be confused with the gun-toting Chinese soldiers.

Dawn is a royal procession moving slowly across the land. At daybreak the mountain peaks, first to receive the light, sparkle like clusters of gems. The valley below changes color, with cold blues lifting out of the dark browns. Then from the pit of the valley a fog mushrooms, obscuring the lower region until the sun bakes the air. The absolute beauty inspires me, and I let fly my pink-headed duck call.

"What was that?" asks a bewildered Sonam. "Is it part of your daily devotions?"

I explain. He wants to give the call a try, and when I tell him that the sound should embody a dream quality, he nods. He trills something quite exotic in its own way, but far different from my call. As I correct him, the forest erupts with chirping sounds; whistling thrushes and collared bushchats respond and wing their way toward us.

I take out a camera to shoot a picture of Sonam with a thrush in the background.

"No photographs!" he scolds me. "If something happens, the police will be able to locate everything and everybody. No cameras until Tibet."

I remind him of our agreement allowing unrestricted use of cameras, tape recorders, and notebooks.

"Things change," he tells me. "You can write all you want, but no cameras."

The camera goes back into the bag. It's not worth arguing about; we'll let Sonam's teacher decide the issue. I keep quiet as we walk on.

"I thought you said it was four or five miles to the house," I pant between breaths. We've already covered seven or eight miles, and at this altitude each step is a woeful reminder that I should quit smoking.

"Not far now," Sonam replies.

We continue, my bag growing heavier by the step. At last we reach a gravel path flanked by stately pines.

"This is it," Sonam chimes as he starts trotting up the incline, leaving me far behind.

I follow at a steady pace, my lungs heaving like a bellows. The trail leads to a large wooden building with golden ornaments on the roof. They are *chortens* — relic holders and statues of worship. From a distance a chorten appears conical, but up close I see the customary four forms stacked one atop the other. The rectangular base represents earth; the circle above it signifies water, which cleanses; the triangle on that evokes fire and its ability to purify; and the ellipse on top denotes ether, capping the three elements as it does the heavens. The roofline arcs with the mountainscape, sweeping upward at the ends to touch the distant summits. The walls, soft gray surfaces, seem to absorb my image as I stare at them.

The front door opens, and Sonam, full of energy, bounds out. He embraces me and leads me inside. Clouds of perfumed smoke hang in the front room. The plastered walls are richly decorated with religious paintings and sculpture. The incense has an intoxicating effect; I find it hard to stop grinning and must concentrate to subdue the feeling of giddiness.

Two young boys enter the room carrying bowls of fruit. Their heads are shaved and they wear the maroon and saffron robes of the priesthood. They stare at me wide-eyed; perhaps I'm the first westerner they've seen. Sonam introduces them:

"These are students who will be great lamas someday. Right?"

Embarrassed, they look down at their feet. Sonam repeats himself.

"Yes, Holy One," they reply, standing tall.

I reach out to shake their hands, but this custom is new to them. Sonam comes to the rescue, saying something in Tibetan, and the boys grab my hand awkwardly.

We walk down a corridor lit by oil lamps. Bronze incense braziers in the shape of bird's nests exude different fragrances, some sweet and others pungent. We near a doorway leading into the kitchen, where three women are preparing food. Seeing me, they fall silent. Sonam talks quickly to them and pulls me away from the kitchen. We stop in front of a massive teak door inscribed with the Wheel of Life. Sonam knocks and lifts the latch without waiting for a response. I brush my shoes on the backs of my pant legs.

No natural light comes into the room because the windows and walls are covered with heavy maroon brocade. Candles are massed at one end, flickering in long tiered rows. Overhead a pattern of golden lotus blossoms floats on a ceiling covered in blood-red silk. Three bronze statues of Buddha sit on an altar spanning the front of the room. The candlelight animates their faces, and Buddha's eyes seem to follow me.

Three lamas are sitting in the lotus position with their backs to us. Their long hair is braided and curled atop their heads, the braids held in place by strands of crimson yarn. The priest in the center stops chanting and rises to his feet. The other two men, both dressed in maroon, follow his example. He glides toward me, his arms outstretched, his hands invisible under the voluminous sleeves of white silk.

"Welcome," he says in heavily accented English. "Welcome to our home."

Like his hair, his eyes are quite dark. I guess his age at forty. "You must be tired after your long trip," he says, embracing me. "Has Sonam been a good host?"

"Never a dull moment, Holy One."

"Please, there is no need to be formal. You may call me friend." (This is a courteous gesture, but I address him as His Holiness or Master, like everyone else.)

He waves at the boys, who bow, leave the room, and return carrying a golden urn and a silver tray with two pieces of bread on it. I follow Sonam's example and swallow a pellet of dough. His Holiness sprinkles our heads with sacred water before pouring some of it into our palms. Again like Sonam, I drink a little before snorting several drops. Later I'm told that this ensures that the blessing will reach both the heart and the mind.

The master finishes the ritual and leads us into a bright, sunlit room with a flower-laden table in the center. As in Ganju Lama's house, simple wooden chairs line the walls.

"You must be hungry," His Holiness says, pointing to a seat on his right. Sonam sits to his left, and the boys take their places next to him. The women bring out bowls of hot food and sit next to me. The delicious aroma reminds me that my last meal was more than a day ago. However, no one eats. I hold back too, assuming that the others are praying, not realizing that they're staring at me and not into their hearts.

His Holiness touches my wrist and gently informs me that the guest must start the meal. My first bite sends the others digging into their bowls. The porridge is sweet and heavily spiced with cinnamon. I eat slowly, pausing between mouthfuls to contemplate something odd. For several seconds after His Holiness touched me, my wrist felt hot. Is he such a master of Tumo that he can instantly conjure heat? Or are his fingertips coated with something caustic? I have many things to ask him when the time is right.

There's no conversation at the table, and the boys wolf down their servings of porridge, bowls of rice, steamed vegetables, bread, yak butter, and yak milk. When we've finished, the master and the two other priests excuse themselves, returning to their prayers, and Sonam escorts me to my room. Normally talkative, he now barely speaks. We will be leaving in two days, but the exact timetable won't be set until tomorrow.

"Will you tell me the name of that village?" I ask, pointing out the window at some distant buildings.

"You must ask the master these questions," he replies curtly.

It is not a time to argue — both of us are tired — and we agree to get some sleep. The soporific effect of the food is stayed momentarily by the splendid view of Mount Kanchenjunga. Today the god is dressed in all its glory: the peak rising above ermine clouds, a shaft of golden light piercing the left side of the Lord of Earth and Snow.

The cozy room is decorated with scenes from the life of Buddha, alias Siddhartha Gautama, a.k.a. The Great One, or simply The Lotus Born. Visions of Buddha flow through my deep and dreamy rest. I'm listening to him preach under the Tree of Knowledge when Sonam wakes me. He's off to retrieve the car, but I'm to remain here. "The fewer people who see you, the safer our trip."

Before leaving, he shows me to the rooftop bath, which turns out to be an eight-foot cast-iron tub. Near the drain I notice a raised emblem: "Bristol, 1879." Somehow this enormous tub traveled more than 15,000 miles before landing here; it must have been a Herculean task hauling it through the mountains to Sikkim.

After finding a towel and retrieving my binoculars, I pull the brass chain, and hot water fills the tub from a string of black goat skins dangling from a bamboo pole above it. I slip into the water and experience instant satisfaction. The rooftop offers a panoramic view of endless azure and white space. With my binoculars, I watch Sonam and the boys lugging jerry cans. Beyond them I see a small village with several ponies and bullock carts on the main street. If this is Lachen, its famous monastery should be visible, but it isn't. The town must be either Lachung or Yumthang. To the south lie poison-green valleys bounded by steep mountains frosted with snow; to the east is the Donkha Range, the Himalayan spur that forms the boundary between Tibet and Bhutan; to the north is one of the uncharted regions, a white blank on my maps and possibly the home of the pink-headed duck.

I lie naked in the tepid water, basking in the afternoon light. A group of bulbuls flies overhead. The sun flashes about their cobalt heads and white cheeks. I hear a woodpecker, but I can't see it. There are no ducks in sight, not even a common red pochard. I inhale deeply and quack, hoping a reclusive duck will hear me. The swallows in the trees scatter; the woodpecker falls silent.

Dried and refreshed, I wander around the house, poking my head into each of the four large bedrooms. All of the chambers are lavishly adorned with religious objects. Buddhists use art, or *yantras,* to focus the cosmic forces of the visual world, much as they use mantras to channel the energies of sound. Self-expression has little role in Himalayan Buddhist art. It's not forbidden, but little purpose is seen in it.

On the ground floor most of the tapestries recreate a familiar scene of Buddha surrounded by deer, which symbolize his first sermon in Varanasi's Deer Park. My tour ends abruptly when I collide with one of the Lepcha women, overturning her bucket. She goes into the kitchen, fetches a mop, and glares as she thrusts it my way. She doesn't have to speak, and I get right to work. Lepcha women are not to be argued with. In their society they hold the dominant role. In conjugal matters they are the sole arbiters of justice; they may have extramarital affairs, but their husbands must remain monogamous.

His Holiness and the two older lamas appear just as I finish cleaning up the puddle. The master looks puzzled but asks me to join him and his teachers. For ten hours a day, every day since his fifth birthday, his life has been devoted to learning.

"These holy men tutor me in history, politics, and languages. They also instruct me in the lessons of the spirit."

"Isn't ten hours a day a bit much?" I ask as we sit down in front of the teachers, both of whom have long, wispy beards.

"Oh, no! There is so much to learn . . . If I close my eyes or stare at a *thanka* [wall hanging], I can be alone. Is this not the same for you?"

"As you say, Holiness, there's much to learn."

The boys bring us tea, and he mentions some of the books he has read, many of them Western classics, including works by Cervantes and Shakespeare. His knowledge of political history is impressive, as is his fluency in nine languages. At the moment he's studying Portuguese and admits to having trouble with all of its irregular verbs. While we talk, the teachers continue to murmur in low voices, reading from books. I suppose that through osmosis some of what they say seeps into the master's head.

He tells me that his dream is of a free Tibet, and he has dedicated the past few years to that goal. The Dalai Lama, who is the head of another sect, and he work closely together on most matters.

"The Dalai Lama knows nothing about this trip into Tibet," he says, taking my hand in his. "We must not implicate him." He closes his eyes and keeps his hand in mine. I feel as if he's staring at me, and I ask whether he's worried that we may be caught.

"Caution is a virtue, don't you agree?" he says, opening his eyes.

"Sonam doesn't want me taking pictures. I promised to ask you for permission."

"Save your film for Guru." He lets go of my hand and picks up a string of prayer beads. The teachers close their books and start chanting softly, "Om mani padme hoummm." His Holiness joins in, but I have more questions and ask him to indulge me.

"Sonam talked about a dream both of you had about me adrift in the ocean. Is that true?"

"Yes, it is true. We saw you in the water. But Gangtok is a small place, and I knew about you before that night."

He speaks matter-of-factly, as if the dream was not a mystical harbinger of joined destinies, but the result of an investigation of some type. He artfully dodges my questions about his psychic training and powers, reminding me that lamas have no monopoly on telepathy or out-of-body experiences.

"The belief in self is the greatest obstacle on the road to enlightenment," he says, concisely explaining a basic tenet of Buddhism.

"What about the heat on my wrist when we were eating?" I ask, going on to detail the sensation.

"That must have been something you imagined."

"I'm sure I didn't imagine it."

"You must look beyond yourself for the answer," he replies.

The older priests return to their books when they realize that His Holiness has shifted his attention away from his beads. The master and I commune for the next two hours while the teachers read on, sounding like white noise in the background. I discover that he's not particularly interested in my views but is always eager to instruct me in Buddhist thought.

My visions cling to the statistical lifespan of seventy-three years, but his involve eons, cycles of many lifetimes culminating in Nirvana. The narrower and more pointed the question I ask, the more His Holiness resorts to aphorisms, gently chiding me to recognize that many paths lead to the same place. As we end our discussion, he offers one last bit of advice: "Seek an understanding of faith. It will do you good."

He may be right.

Late the next day our two guides arrive. The one named Padam speaks excellent English, and he reports that the death of a Chinese soldier in Lhasa has caused havoc for smugglers and guides. Security patrols are out in force; the Sikkim-Tibet border is sealed. Martial law has been declared in Tibet, and the normal crossing points are now armed camps. Natu-La, Jelep-La, Cho-La — all the mountain passes in the south — are far too dangerous to use now.

"Things change every hour," Padam assures us. "Tomorrow the border may return to normal. Who knows? . . . I always hope for the best."

"What if things get worse?" I ask.

"We wait . . . I hope you play cards."

At last our plans become definite: we will leave at two in the morning, driving and then walking to a safe house, where we will hide during the daylight hours. Once the moon has set, we will strike into Tibet and head directly for Guru, traveling in a car Padam has secured somewhere over the border.

"The only question left, my large American friend, is how you will pass for a hillsman?" Padam says.

I drop my shoulders and bend my knees, slouching into a posture that only inspires alarm. Padam and his friend Phuchung roll their eyes. Sonam claims to have the solution to what he calls my "big problem." I'll impersonate a monk, wearing a maroon robe, a yellow knit hat, and a long scarf.

"You think it will work?" Padam asks, handing me the disguise and helping me dress.

I put on the robe, pull on the hat, and wrap my neck and

face with the scarf. Padam helps adjust the outfit. His hands, covered with callouses, are rough, and when he touches my neck, they feel like sandpaper.

"You look silly," he says, giving up.

"Silly American or silly hillsman?" I quip.

"It doesn't matter," he replies. "If the Chinese see you, it means they have seen us all. We cannot let them get that close . . . The robes will do."

We will have to carry our own food and gear; Padam insists that we avoid villages, trusting only other smugglers. "Who knows what threats the Chinese have made against the villagers. Only outlaws are safe."

"Then everything is ready!" Sonam exclaims, rising from his chair.

"Good . . . We leave tonight," Padam declares.

His Holiness summons us for a final blessing, asking the spirit of the universe to protect us on this holy mission.

"May Tibet be free," he intones, sprinkling water on us.

He gives each of the others a prayer scarf and a kiss on the forehead, then turns to me.

"This is for your safe entry," he says, draping a silk scarf around my shoulders.

He repeats the rite with another scarf and says, "This is for your safe return."

Surprisingly, he pulls out a third scarf, which he blesses several times. "This scarf you will give to someone. The image is coming to you now." The face of a friend I haven't seen in years emerges.

The master touches my left shoulder and tells me to close my eyes while he and the teachers pray in a low drone. Streams of incense envelop me. For a moment I feel as if I'm being lifted by the smoke. His Holiness touches me again and tells me to open my eyes. From under the stack of prayer scarves he withdraws an ivory box, which he opens slowly. Inside is an ordinary-looking piece of wood.

"This is the Tree of Life, handed from father to son, believer to believer," he says, showing us one of the most sacred relics in Buddhism, a piece of the Bodhi Tree.

"For forty days the Great One sat under this wood while meditating and fighting temptation . . . Behold the Tree of Life, the Tree of Knowledge, the Tree of Buddha . . ."

His Holiness invites me to pry loose a splinter. While he holds the sacred wood, I gently dig a knife into it, raising a sliver. It slips through my fingers to the ground. Sonam gasps and dives to retrieve the precious relic.

"This is great power," he thunders, handing back the talisman.

His Holiness concludes the ceremony by chanting 108 times, "Om mani padme houm."

The boys lead us from the inner sanctum to the front room. Padam and Phuchung sidle up to me, and for the first time I feel that I'm an asset to our expedition.

"Even the master knows we need luck . . . Can I see the charms?" Padam asks. I hand him the silk pouch His Holiness has given me to protect the relic. There are also some stones and bits of colored glass inside, each blessed to protect me against particularly powerful devils. Padam looks them over and nods his head approvingly.

"His Holiness has told me a little about you," he says. "You came all the way from America to find a bird? Is that right?"

"Yes, do you know anything about birds?"

"Only what I learned in the army. Birds are what we called girls."

"British Gurkha?"

"Yes, sir," he says snapping to attention. "Commando. Sixth Regiment. Queen's Own Guard. Retired."

We talk about our forthcoming expedition.

"I told His Holiness last week that we had to move quickly," Padam says. "It will start snowing soon and then the passes will be closed until spring. It is now or next year for this trip.

They had to get somebody in a hurry, so I guess it was you."

"Ah," I say, finally understanding my role as a convenient eyewitness for the west.

Sonam rejoins us, carrying a pitcher of hot yak's milk from the kitchen. We all sip a glass, hoping to sleep during the four hours until departure. My drowsiness ends the moment I lie down. My heart pounds as I think about crossing the border, and when Sonam knocks on my door later, I haven't slept at all.

Much to my relief, Phuchung takes over the driving. Constantly shifting, accelerating into the turns, and concentrating entirely on the road, he handles the car like a pro. We motor for nearly three hours and finally stop behind a tumbledown shack that belongs to one of Padam's cousins.

"Hurry!" Padam says in a hushed voice, pointing to another building almost invisible in the darkness. As we unload the gear, he admonishes, "Please, try to be quiet."

We make our way along a narrow path leading to Dachi-La, a high-altitude pass in northeastern Sikkim. The pace is slow, but after several hours my shoes feel like anvils. Sonam offers to carry my bag, but I refuse; he's already lugging much of our food: fifteen kilos of flour, rice, beans, and biscuits. Padam and Phuchung are also hauling heavy loads, contents unknown.

I tote my bag like a backpack, straps over my shoulders, while the others carry their burdens in wicker baskets, straps around their foreheads, letting their neck and head muscles take the strain. As I huff and puff, barely managing to keep up, the guides chat and drag on cigarettes.

"You should see the view during the day . . . Gordama Lake, Lahmo Lake, Bam, Lachog . . . beautiful, beautiful view," Padam says in a lilting voice.

At the moment I have an intense headache and find it hard to imagine that anything is beautiful. I stroke my charms, hoping they will disperse the demons pounding my temples. At last we leave the path and cut through some brambles to a small yak-skin hut, one of Padam and Phuchung's hideouts.

"Usually we store cargo here, but today you will also stay here . . . We still have a long way to the top. You should rest."

I need no further encouragement. Five aspirins chase away most of the pain, and I fall asleep. When I awake, the sun is shining on Sonam saying his prayers. He interrupts his devotions to explain that Padam and Phuchung have gone to talk to friends, including some contacts in the army.

As much as I want to inspect the flora and fauna, I keep my promise not to wander from the yurt. By lunchtime the guides are back with grim news: both armies have increased their patrols over the past twenty-four hours.

"We will have to wait," Padam says. "What's your favorite card game?"

If the Chinese ever invade India again, they will most likely use the southern crossings, those closest to the oil fields and paved roads. For this reason fewer soldiers are posted here at Dachi-La. While Padam and Phuchung use several passes for business, smuggling mostly cigarettes and salep into Tibet, Dachi-La is their favorite. They have established what Padam calls an "understanding" with the border troops, but during a military alert all deals are suspended.

Sonam impatiently asks how long we will have to wait. Padam isn't sure, a response that vexes the lama. Sonam begins speaking rapidly in Tibetan, emphasizing certain words by stomping his foot. Phuchung turns away, shrugs his shoulders, and starts dealing a hand of cards. Sonam knocks away the cards and draws a stick furiously across the ground, making crude diagrams as he speaks. Phuchung reshuffles and deals another hand.

"Rummy?" he asks, discarding.

Padam has been listening politely to Sonam, whose voice is rising. Eventually, Padam throws up his arms.

"Stop," he says to Sonam. "Forget it. The American cannot go. None of us can go right now."

There's no argument from me. I've never crossed a Himalayan mountain pass, and I'm not eager to make my first attempt under less than ideal conditions.

"Let the American stay here and take me, just me . . . I will use his cameras," Sonam says without looking my way.

"What?" I ask.

"It is your responsibility . . . Give me the cameras. This is for a free Tibet . . . You must, you *have* to give me the cameras."

"No way." I didn't come here to sit and play cards for three days in the cold.

Padam steps between us and speaks to Sonam. "Even if the American gives you his cameras, who will lead you across? Phuchung and I are going to stay here. We will wait until tomorrow."

"Ha!" Sonam taunts. "You the great warrior, the famous guide . . . are you afraid of the Chinese dogs?"

"That is right," Padam says directly into my tape recorder. "That is why I am still alive."

After a half hour of bickering, it's agreed that Padam and Sonam will return to the house of His Holiness and seek his advice. We will abide by the wishes of the master. I will even surrender one of my cameras if he so instructs.

Phuchung and I pass the time by playing cards, pitching coins (though we both cheat, he always wins), and going through my survival gear. He's especially fascinated by my slingshot, and after an hour of practice he's a better marksman than I. A fire might disclose our presence, so we eat cold biscuits and chocolate for dinner. I retire early and awake the next day to Padam's gentle nudging.

"Time to get up, soldier," he says, throwing open the flap of the yurt. "Sun is up."

His Holiness has canceled our trip, he tells me, and Sonam has remained at the house. It seems that his blind determination disturbed His Holiness. Padam suspects that they will try to corral another westerner in the spring. Phuchung starts gathering the gear for the trek back down the path.

"Can't we wait and try again in a couple of days?" I ask.

"No," Padam replies emphatically. "I promised to take you to Siliguri."

"Did you say when?"

"No. Why?"

"I've got an idea," I say dipping into my bag for the illustration. "Remember that duck, the pink one I'm looking for? Here it is." They laugh at the idea, but their eyes light up with my offer to pay for guide services. Tracing the border of the unknown area on my map, I ask them to take me to Yumthang, the last settlement marked on the chart.

"How much will you pay?"

"You tell me."

The two guides confer. Padam speaks for Phuchung. "He wants to know if you really want to do this?"

"That's why I'm here. The duck is part of my dream."

"If you get caught, you know the rules: we don't know you and you don't know us . . . Good. You will have to pay for gas, and let's see . . . How long do you want to go for?"

"A week to ten days."

"Ten days . . . OK, you will have to pay us," he pauses for a moment, "ohhh, that comes to a thousand rupees each plus expenses."

"Deal," I agree, after calculating the dollar value ($130 plus).

Three hours later we're on the road to Yumthang in the Rover, which His Holiness has loaned Padam and Phuchung until he moves to another monastery. As we bounce along, I cradle my charms; their power seems to be working. In a burst of exuberance, I wish out loud for a beer. The Rover slams to a stop.

"Will you buy?" Padam asks.

Phuchung swings the car around and drives as fast as he can. We pull up to a small farm and start honking. Two cows stop chewing to stare at us, and the chickens scatter. The farmhouse appears to be made from bits and pieces of every kind of grass and tree growing at this altitude. The front door cracks open and an old man peers out suspiciously. Padam sticks his head out the car window and says something in Lepcha. I stay behind while they "conduct business." Moments later I hear laughter and the clinking of glasses, sounds that continue for the next hour. Finally Padam and Phuchung return with armloads of assorted bottles, some big, some small, some green, most clear, and all containing beer. Like the bottles, the caps have been used before, and it takes some doing to pry them loose. I take my first sip just as the Rover hits a rut, and the beer foams and sprays all over me. It has a tangy taste, as if orange peels were added years ago, as well as a hint of ginger. The aftertaste has the bite of cardamom. Whatever, it's delicious.

After a few bottles, Padam starts loosening up, telling me local legends about the uncharted area, supposed home of man-beasts and spirits.

"If you do not find that duck, maybe you will see Me-Gu! If you are very lucky, it will chase you all the way into the Valley of Bliss," he says, laughing.

Me-Gu, better known in the west as the Abominable Snowman, is just as real to Padam and Phuchung as the Himalayan black bear or the snow leopard, rare species that few people have actually seen. The Valley of Bliss is a place of intoxicating beauty and serenity. When a hillsman wanders from his camp and never returns, it's believed that he has found that sacred valley.

"If we only knew where it was, we would go and never return. They say it is in the rhododendron forest," Padam speculates between gulps.

"We both have friends who have seen Me-Gu. Not far from Yumthang . . . Do not believe stories about it attacking people. It runs when it sees people."

Phuchung digs into his pocket, pulls out a small leather bag, and shows me the special charm that protects him from Me-Gu.

Me-Gu is thought to be a human being whose body has been possessed by a devil. If Padam or Phuchung ever sees one, he will run to a lama as quickly as possible. Although the charm keeps the devil at bay, only the incantations formulated by the wizard-priest Guru Rimpoche, the eighth-century mystic and founder of Lamaism, can purge the believer of the effects of Me-Gu's evil eye. As I carry the holiest, most powerful charms either of them have seen, they're certain we're safe from all devils.

However, I'm not safe from soldiers or the loose tongues of villagers. Phuchung will check with a relative in Yumthang about hiring a donkey to carry my food and gear.

"I would go with you, but I have a girlfriend in Yumthang," Padam boasts.

"Were you planning to come here anyway?" I ask.

"It was none of your business," he says with a smile.

A couple of miles from Yumthang, Phuchung drops me off in a thickly wooded area. They will go into town to make arrangements for the donkey. When they reappear two hours later, it sounds as if a parade is approaching. The Rover's horn is tooting and both of them are singing.

"Sounds like your duck, eh?" Padam yells. "Quack quack quack!" He hands me another beer while Phuchung blasts out a tempo with the horn. "Honk! Honk-honk-honk! Honk!"

"Stop. Stop it!" I plead, a hangover already setting in. "I thought we were supposed to be quiet."

"You are the one who must be quiet, not us," Padam replies, quacking as Phuchung beeps again.

They've found Phuchung's relatives, Padam's girlfriend, and another smuggler willing to rent his donkey for an exorbitant price.

"It comes with food," Padam consoles as I hand over the money.

They cover me with a tarp, and we drive through town, making our way slowly as they stop to chat with friends. Later Padam tells me that "the people around here think India is a foreign country. Most of them have never seen a plainsman. Just speak Hindi if you have bad luck and happen to meet anyone."

On the other side of town I get out and once again hide in a thicket while they retrieve the donkey. As the afternoon drifts by, I become increasingly anxious, worried that they've gotten so drunk that they've forgotten me or can't drive. I search my Tibetan phrase book for an appropriately angry greeting. Unfortunately, the text is suited only for polite conversation, lacking essential slang and swearwords. The most appropriate sentence I can construct is "Your rates are expensive and service poor, dogs in the street." I've just memorized it when I hear the *clop-clop* of a four-legged animal. I drop behind a bush.

"Duck Man. Oh, Duck Man," I hear Padam hooting in a sing-song voice. "Where, oh, where is the Duck Man?"

"Right here," I shout, adding my Tibetan sentence.

"Been studying, huh? . . . Here, let me tell you some really bad words," he says, rattling off a few. As Padam nears, the smell of liquor overpowers even the odor of the donkey. Phuchung, right on his heels, parks the Rover between us. They help me unload the supplies, advising me to take more food than I had planned on.

"You never know what might happen," Padam chuckles.

Donning the robes and hat of a lama, I become the only six-foot-two-inch monk in Sikkim. The three of us walk down a path leading to a stream, pulling the donkey along. When we are past the spot where villagers bathe, we stake out a campsite. After showing me how to hobble, feed, and pack the donkey, Padam suggests an itinerary: "Follow the stream for several days and then take a left. Come back the same way, and we will meet here in eight days."

"That's it?" I say incredulously.

He assures me that the army is nowhere near. The trail along the stream is rarely used by villagers. If I encounter anyone, it will be a yak herder or Me-Gu.

"Remember, be careful. I promised His Holiness to deliver you safely to Siliguri."

We agree that I should leave a strip of yellow fabric at my campsites and at the turn up to the steppes toward the rhododendron forest. As the two of them leave, Phuchung whispers to Padam, who translates: "He wants to know if you are scared?"

"Yes."

"Good. Stay that way and you will be OK . . . Goodnight, Duck Man."

5

Into the Valley of Bliss

ABOVE ME the moon begins its swing across an ebony sky. Draco and Lyra dot the northern horizon, Gemini and Orion lie to the east. The tall pines are motionless, and my breath hangs in the chill air. The soft murmuring of the river spirit puts me at ease.

I build a small fire, keeping the flames low. Any strong aromas will attract the village dogs, so I eat a spare meal of biscuits and tea. As I climb under my blankets of yak hair and nettle fiber, I wish I had brought my hot-water bottle.

I decamp before dawn and scoot ahead of any village bather or wood gatherer. The donkey seems willing to follow me. She is quite small, standing about four feet at the shoulder, but her long ears make her appear taller. Padam forgot to tell me her name, and in an uninspired moment I dub her "Partner." My only other experience with a pack animal was years ago in North Africa while traveling along the edge of the Sahara searching for a rare desert bloom. That beast, a mule, was nasty and foul-tempered. I named it Monster.

During the monsoon season this branch of the Tista is a raging torrent that claws at its banks and climbs into the forest, at war with anything trying to contain it. But now, well into the dry season, the river is less than a fifth of its full size. The high-water mark, where trees have been stripped of branches, is clearly visible above me.

Despite Padam's assurances that the trail is rarely used, I'm still worried about being spotted by a villager. I rush along, trying to put distance between me and Yumthang. My paranoia fades as the shadows lengthen. The combination of fatigue, acclimation, and impending darkness finally slows my pace.

Ahead I notice a Himalayan pied kingfisher hovering over the water. Taking several deep breaths, I summon its distant cousin.

"Q-U-A-C-K, quack, quar-o-whack!"

"Hee-haw. Hee-haw," Partner brays.

The kingfisher darts into the trees, its speckled black-and-white plumage blending with the bark. A jungle myna lets out a cry from somewhere inside the evergreens. Indian moorhens join in, drowning out the myna with their tinny call: "Careek-crek-rek."

Partner and I keep an eye out for a suitable place to sleep. The sun sets early here. Rather than slipping behind a remote horizon, it impales itself on the towering Himalayan spurs. Just before darkness the mountains, ringed by light, appear to ignite, sparking thousands of Saint Elmo's fires. As I watch the last traces of color glaze the left bank of the river, I'm drawn to a dark shape among the boulders — the entrance to a cave. There are no tracks around, but to be certain I don't startle a sleeping mountain cat or bear, I bark loudly and toss a few stones into the opening. Nothing growls or crawls out, so I poke my head inside and turn on a flashlight. The cave reverberates with the sound of flapping wings.

Whap, whap, whap, whap . . . whoosh! whoosh!

Two Himalayan leaf-nosed bats fly out, sending me to the ground. Though my field guide says they're harmless, the leaf-nosed are the largest and most frightening of Indian bats. Their faces, the color of raw umber, look devilish, with ears shaped like horns. Their name is derived from the membrane of their noses, an organ that detects the slightest variation in sound waves.

I unload Partner, who has remained quiet throughout the excitement. Tonight, as a reward for her docile behavior, I give her a double helping of food. There's plenty of driftwood for a fire, and with a few whacks of my machete, I cut enough pine boughs for a mattress. Dinner is rice, lentils, and onions, with a dessert of a chocolate bar and one cigarette, only my third of the day. At sea level a pack a day barely keeps my hands from jittering, but at this altitude my thirst for nicotine has waned drastically.

When I awaken the next morning, my pink-headed duck call echoes down the river canyon. "Scree-scree," wail kingfishers on the wing; spotted babblers trill; and a pair of racket-tailed drongos, with their shiny plumage and two long cobalt tail feathers, respond with a metallic clicking, "Kapock-tanka-tanka." Alas, no quacks.

Partner and I forge onward as the red morning sky turns to slate. Cumulonimbus clouds pile up, riding the van of a cold front. Feeling certain that the nearly dry riverbed will contain the rainfall without flooding, I follow its edge, climbing the bank to circumvent giant boulders or steep inclines. Thickening clouds blot out the mountaintops as the rain begins. At first it's a gentle drizzle, but then the wind kicks up, shaking loose whatever leaves remain on the trees, and it begins to pour. Water splatters against the rocks and pounds the underbrush. Only the spirit of the river enjoys this change in the weather, roaring its song to Mount Kanchenjunga. My poncho becomes useless, and soon I'm as drenched as Partner. After I stumble a third time and fall hard on my shoulder, we squeeze into a rock hollow protected by an overhang. Throughout the afternoon and well into the night, the gale rages. Partner and I huddle together, shivering in the wet air.

In the morning I awake with a start. It's a beautiful day, not a cloud in sight, but where's Partner? Frantic, I search about and find her about a kilometer away, grazing happily alongside a brook. More interested in eating watercress than heeding my commands, she refuses to budge. I decide that if she won't follow me, I'll just have to follow her. To reach the rhododendrons and the uncharted region, we have to leave the stream at some point anyway, and this seems as good a spot as any.

Cartography has never been my strong point. A professor of geography, reviewing some maps I had drawn of a region in Africa, concluded: "Terra incognita is safe in your hands." I can plot a position across any ocean, but my grasp of land measure seems infirm. A good orienteer frequently sights with a compass, triangulating positions, gridding the terrain into blocks, but I'm far too lazy to do this. Pinpoint accuracy matters little to me. As long as we're traveling toward the unknown, we're on the right track.

As we climb skyward, the forest dwindles into clusters of weeping spruce trees, their limbs mostly gnarled and stunted. The underbrush, generally elder and what looks like honeysuckle, gives way to the starkness of the steppes. Brownish yellow grass crackles underfoot, each stem as brittle as raw spaghetti, and blankets of moss and lichen cover the rocks. Now, in late autumn, the wildflowers are all past; ahead is the snow line, a pristine mantle draped across the Himalayas.

On we go, Partner and I, marching across trackless land, up and down the innumerable valleys until my legs ache. I don't see any birds the entire day, but that night I hear a strange call, like a cross between a loon and a screech owl, which I can't identify.

The morning marks my fourth on the trail, the midpoint of my tramp. By my reckoning the giant rhododendron forest is less than five kilometers away, and undoubtedly the Valley of Bliss is nearby. Me-Gu may be watching me brush my teeth. The pink-headed duck could be anywhere.

While combing the area for kindling, I hear a voice, but it's so soft that I dismiss it as my imagination and go on about my business. But the voice calls again, and this time I answer, "Hell-o. Who's that?"

"Ah, hell-o, my friend," a man says in Hindi as he steps from behind a large rock. His beard reaches to his slender waist. He walks toward me with outstretched hands.

"Welcome," he says, clasping my arms.

"Who are you?" I ask, startled.

"An old man doing penance," he replies in perfect English.

He's shoeless and wears a threadbare robe, yet the early morning cold doesn't seem to affect him. His eyes are deep-set, rounder than those of a hillsman, and his skin is dark, suggesting family roots in southern India.

"Englishman, yes?" he asks.

"American. Would you like a shawl, or something to eat?"

"No, thank you. I have all I need."

I invite him to share tea and a meal with me. Instead he points northward and tells me that his home is close by. I quickly load Partner and we head off. I'm full of questions, but the old man asks for silence.

"Let us enjoy the first light," he says. "If you listen closely you will hear the world awake. It is my favorite time of day."

After we have walked for half an hour, the outline of the giant rhododendron forest looms above us, a black smudge on the horizon. The closer we get, the more immense and imposing it becomes. At last, I touch a leaf, making contact with one of nature's grandest spectacles. Towering over my head are the largest rhododendrons of the world, the *giganteum* species, each as big as an American ranch house. It's long past their flowering season, but a few stubborn, wilted blossoms remain. The leaves, almost a foot long, are a glossy kelly green with velvety brown undersides.

"Please," says my guide, motioning toward a small lean-to. "My home. Consider it yours."

The rickety structure is an adequate windbreak but offers little protection from rain or cold. I glance about his camp, noting that his worldly belongings — a small wooden bowl, a spoon, a kettle, a pot, and a tin cup — could fit inside my camera bag. His bed is a layer of grass and leaves. Hanging in the corner is a beautifully embroidered sash, which my host tells me is a *somthag,* or meditation sash. By tying it under his knees and around his head, he can remain in the lotus position for days on end.

"Make yourself comfortable," he says, sitting down on a nest of branches near the campfire.

I offer some tea, and he talks while filling the kettle. It seems many eyes have been watching me since I left the river course. The yak herders have been tracking me with great interest. The strange combination of my dress, size, and skin color has bewildered them. They are unsure if I'm a lama or a devil. Should I be revered or stoned? They have asked the holy man for advice.

"I promised to protect them if you were a devil . . . From their description, I knew you had to be lost."

Usually, when a devil possesses a human, the body changes, becoming distorted and hairy like Me-Gu; however, the most powerful devils can slip in without radically changing their host's appearance. These disguised devils can then enter a hut and attack its inhabitants, spreading disease and causing death. The locals believe that sickness is caused by either a curse or an evil spirit, so there will be trouble if someone falls ill while I'm in the region.

"Wear your cap at all times," the mystic advises. "Cover as much of yourself as possible."

"I'm not here to interfere," I say, assuring him of my good intentions.

"You have interfered already . . . Stories will be told about you long after you leave."

He arches his eyebrows and trains his eyes on my forehead. I wonder if he's reading my thoughts and ask him if he's a lung-gom-pa.

He doesn't answer, and I query, "Gompchen? Or are you a nal-jor-pa?" Of all lamas, the gompchens are considered the most adept at conjuring mystical forces. It is said that they can release their spirit at will from the confinement of the body and escape the material world. The nal-jor-pas are magicians endowed with varying powers; the best-trained can cast fatal spells.

"I am nothing more than an old man doing penance."

"But you do practice Tumo, don't you?" I say, pointing at his bare feet. Novitiates in Tumo are required to pass a test; they are wrapped in a wet sheet at an altitude above 12,000 feet and must generate enough body heat to dry the sheet in a matter of minutes.

"Ah, you know about Tumo and gompchens?"

"Very little, but I would like to know more."

"It is the same for me. Now let me ask you a question. Why do you write in your book all the time? Can you not remember?"

"It's a habit. I can stop if you want."

"No, keep writing," he says, standing up in an effortless motion and excusing himself to finish his morning prayers.

I tend to Partner, brushing her coat with a comb given to me as a joke by a friend in Gangtok. When the mystic returns to the fire, he declines breakfast, explaining that he eats only one meal a day. Berries and edible roots are his main diet. Occasionally the yak herders bring him barley flour and some tea. There's always wood from the rhododendron forest to keep a fire blazing, and the brook is only fifty yards away.

"Do you see the yak herders much?" I ask, hoping they keep their distance.

"They respect my solitude, but a lama is needed for horoscopes and at times of death."

When a herdsman dies, he tells me, the body must not be disturbed until the lama arrives. The manner of death and the position of the corpse are important for the formulation of the last rites. First the priest commands the spirit to quit the body and sever its attachments to this world. He then plucks several hairs from the head of the deceased to provide a vent for the spirit's escape. Afterward he draws the horoscope of the dead to determine the most auspicious date of burial or cremation. Until then the body is kept in a seated position inside the family home and treated as if alive.

"Please stay the night," he says. "We have been brought together for a reason . . . will you join me in prayer?"

From the pocket of his robe the mystic draws a *totreng*, a rosary of miniature skulls carved from 108 separate human skulls. It is said that a *totreng* is able to invoke the spirit of each of the deceased. He patiently corrects my posture so that I can assume the lotus position without pain. He tells me to relax, coaching my breathing, explaining that tension can be released every time I exhale. I begin to feel the air circulate inside me. The muscles in my back unknot, as if I'm being massaged. However, try as I might to sustain this feeling, I tighten the moment he stops instructing me. When I'm left to my own devices, relaxation comes from alcohol, smoke, music, books, and female companionship. I finally gather enough courage to admit this.

"Ah, you are a flesh eater, eh?" he says with a smirk.

I tell him how refreshing it is to hear a joke from a lama. After my experiences with Sonam and His Holiness, I assumed all lamas were deadly serious. The mystic is taken aback when I mention His Holiness, whom he knew as a child. At this point I mention my hopes of finding the Valley of Bliss and of sighting Me-Gu, as well as the pink-headed duck. He asks me to describe each of my goals, prodding me with his searching eyes whenever I pause. I show him the picture of the pink duck.

He looks at the bird and says, "I hope you find your duck." His eyes glance upward, noting the position of the sun. A moment later he's off to say his afternoon devotions.

I wait awhile before starting dinner. I'm planning to cook enough rice and lentils to last him a week. While I'm at the brook scooping water into the pot, a shriek pierces the air. It's a frightening sound, like the cry of an animal caught in a trap. Again the noise cuts the air, and this time I locate its source. Perched on the crown of a rhododendron is a great Indian hornbill, almost four feet in length. I run to get my cameras.

The holy man follows me and sights a second hornbill in another rhododendron. Though they prefer the jungles, they're occasional visitors around here, he tells me. Both birds start calling. I'm still twenty yards away when they take off, thrusting their casqued beaks upward, flapping their giant black-and-white wings, rustling the air.

The sun sets as I wait for the hermit to return from his prayers. Dinner has been ready for several hours when I notice him standing on the other side of the fire. The flames appear to lap his robe, and in their light he looks ghostly. From my angle his feet don't seem to touch the ground. As he circles the fire, the amber light causes his gray beard to appear blond. He eases himself onto the ground beside me and begins telling me about Me-Gu.

"Once," he tells me, "I was traveling down the mountain to visit a sick man. People ran from the sight of me. They shouted Me-Gu! Me-Gu! Then a kind man gave me these robes."

He eats very little rice before resuming his prayers. I stare into the fire and continue munching, wondering about Me-Gu. The first recorded sighting occurred in 1887, less than fifty miles from here. The guides of the Englishman Lawrence Waddell pointed out the giant footprints, but Me-Gu remained an obscure mountain beast until 1920, when it was christened the Abominable Snowman by a newspaper writer in Calcutta. The clever journalist enhanced the story of a British Everest expedition that had reported seeing "dark forms in the distance."

At dawn the mystic directs me eastward, away from the

pastures of the yak herders and toward the river, my former pathway. I offer him a flashlight as a gift, but he refuses it. I open the silk pouch containing the holy relics and ask him to share a piece of the Bodhi Tree. He protests, but I split off a piece, which I place inside a Ziploc bag. The mystic clutches it, a happy man.

After several hours of following the edge of the rhododendron forest, searching for a natural break or a path into its heart, I stop to rest. A Himalayan mouse hare, a tailless rabbit covered in glossy russet-colored fur, springs from the edge of the forest. It doesn't see me, but when it stops to twitch its nose and catches my scent, it runs for cover.

If a rabbit can enter the forest, I say to myself, so can I. There's no need for a path; I've brought along a machete and a folding saw; I'll blaze my own trail. When I was researching the rhododendrons of Sikkim, I found only one description of an attempt to cut through such a forest. It occurred almost 150 years ago, far to the west of my position. Thomas Hooker, the man who brought rhododendrons to Europe, gave up after two days of what he called in his journal "miserable work . . . the forest is impenetrable." Knowing that the rhododendron forest is less than a mile wide, I calculate that it will take me no more than four hours to reach the other side and another two, possibly three, to retrace my steps.

I hobble Partner and choose a few items of equipment, including a compass, a flashlight, the machete, and a saw. Attaching one end of a fishing line to a rock, I put the spool in my pocket, ready to pay out the line as I go to mark my way back.

Like the rabbit, I zigzag around the large tree limbs near the edge and cover ten feet without trouble, never using my saw. I knock an hour off my estimate. Hooker had to cut a swath big enough for donkeys and more than two dozen porters, but alone I can wiggle through. My confidence is high, even though it takes twenty minutes to travel the next several feet.

It's as dark as night inside the forest. No sunlight penetrates the thick layers of leaves. I'm crawling now, sliding on my back, trying to inch forward without sawing or hacking the wood. Every time I grab a branch, armies of ants drop onto my head and fall down my shirt. I can't see a thing. The flashlight is useless, the branches so close together the beam is blocked inches from my face.

Working by feel, blindly grabbing one branch after another to drag myself along, I lose track of time. Progress is slow, but I remain convinced that it will get easier. Of course, it only gets worse, denser, branches growing closer to the ground. Finally frustrated by one limb that forces me to move laterally, I head back, coiling the fishing line as I go. Take heart, I tell myself, there will be a payoff once the line is measured. As long as I made it halfway through the forest, I can claim to have explored the heart of the world's largest body of rhododendrons.

Partner is waiting, but the sun has gone. According to the markers on the guide line, I traveled a pitiful ninety-three feet in seven hours. I build a bonfire, feeding it with tinder, hoping the flames will have a cathartic effect and chase away the gloom. The burning rhododendron smells like primrose, and the wood cackles as the resin pops and sizzles. Orange cinders zoom toward the Pleiades. Stepping back from the blaze, I assess the achievement of the day: I'm the first New Yorker to be defeated by a forest of *Rhododendron giganteum.* Let the record books take note.

In the morning I head back down the steppes, following a course toward the river. A piece of yellow cotton flickers in the breeze, marking the point where I turn. As I descend, I start picking up speed, dragging Partner along. Running now, I trip and tumble into a crumpled heap. I lie on my back panting, watching the clouds passing over Mount Kanchenjunga. It is said that somewhere on Kanchenjunga and its four attendant peaks mounds of gold, silver, rubies, and emeralds are hidden. Over the years many men have looked for these celestial treasures, and without fail they've been lost in the mountains. Kanchenjunga, god of the gods, deals swiftly and unmercifully with anyone breaking taboo.

We reach the stream about four hours later, and within three kilometers we encounter our old tracks. Downstream a flock of blue-throated barbets, gaudy birds with crimson heads, greets us. The barbets are feverishly pecking at the seeds of a karya gum tree, a rare sight at this altitude. In the distance I hear the screams of a pack of Himalayan monkeys. Their chatter is loud, but my pink-headed duck call silences them. I decide to rest here and watch the birds winging to and from the gum tree. I sight a white-winged ground thrush, a blue rock thrush, blackbirds, and, surprisingly, a pair of large cuckoo shrikes.

The next day I push on to the cave, arriving well after sunset. The bats flap their wings and settle back on the ceiling. I start a fire, feed Partner, and turn my attention to the leeches on my body. Somehow, one or two always escape a body search, lodging in places like the small of my back, unnoticed until they reach the size of small bananas. A pinch of salt on the head and a tug on the tail is a messy but effective way to remove those that are beyond range of a lit cigarette. I lie down to rest for a moment, before preparing dinner, but when I awake it's the next morning.

Since this is my eighth day on the trail and I'm slightly ahead of schedule, I decide to spend the morning lazing in the sun and fishing. My first few casts don't even draw a nibble. I change lures, adding a tuft of hair from Partner's left ear. The new fly looks like a hairy tadpole and spins well.

"Do you know anything about fishing? That will never work!" booms a voice.

"Who's there?" I ask.

"Let me show you how to do it," says Padam, stepping out from behind a tree.

"How did you get here? I never heard a footstep."

"Once I was a good soldier . . . Give me the stick and the line, but take this first."

He holds out a bottle of scotch. One gulp and I'm doubled over, coughing.

"Sip it, my friend, sip it," he says, casting the line, speaking Lepcha to the fish.

No luckier than I, he shortly hands back the gear, saying, "You scared away all the fish."

As we walk to Yumthang, he relates his week of wild boozing and sex, and I ask him why, if he was having such a good time, is he here?

"My friend got tired."

"Phuchung?"

"No, no, my girlfriend got tired of me. She threw me out and Phuchung is with her now."

For Lepcha women, sexual relations are not binding in any way, being considered simply a natural response to a natural desire. When a woman becomes bored, she may seek out another partner. Padam calls his sweetheart "Tigress," and we both wish the best for Phuchung.

The frontier, Padam tells me, is still closed, the troops on alert, and all smuggling on hold.

"We would have played a lot of card games waiting at the pass," he says. "Hey, did you find your duck?"

"I think I was close."

"What?"

"I think it was right in front of me and I missed it."

As we continue walking, the conversation drifts to the Gurkha National Liberation Front. As a hillsman, Padam supports any mountain group struggling against people from the plains. Although he's a Lepcha and a Buddhist, he sympathizes with the Gurkha fight and confides that he has transported materiel across the border for the insurgents. Many of his friends from the army are involved in the battle. He suggests I forget the duck and instead find out more about the Gurkhas.

A mile from Yumthang, Padam scouts the path for villagers before escorting me to my old hiding spot. I'll wait until he returns the donkey and retrieves Phuchung.

Several hours pass before I hear the distinctive rattle of the Land Rover. Padam appears to be alone. Where's Phuchung? Padam lifts the tarp in the back and points to his snoring friend.

"The Tigress has struck . . . Under you go. He will keep you warm."

We drive on through the night. Near the border of West Bengal, Padam stops at a teahouse and pours several hot cups down Phuchung's throat, and he revives enough to climb into the passenger seat. The border police wave us through.

"They probably smelled us coming," Padam quips, noting my woodsy odor and Padam's scent of beer and sex.

Once we cross the border and leave the Darjeeling district, I'm a tourist again and no longer have to hide. We breakfast in Siliguri, or "Sillyugly," as Padam refers to it. At the airport I retrieve my bags from storage and find that there are seats available on the next flight to New Delhi. The plane leaves in thirty minutes, and we hurriedly say good-bye, exchanging addresses and embracing. As I head to the security area, Padam shouts, "Don't forget the duck . . ." He smiles and waves as the customs officer leads me into a separate room.

"Open your bags."

"The plane leaves soon . . ."

"The duck. I want to see the duck."

"If you insist," I respond and take out the illustration. "You see, I'm searching for the pink-headed duck, the rarest . . ."

6

The Grand Life Hotel

THE THIRTY-MINUTE DRIVE from the airport into New Delhi drags on for three hours, yet another lesson in navigation: rely on the numbering system posted above the bus windshield and not the driver. As usual, the brightly lit lobby of the Grand Life Hotel is empty, but the TV room is packed. Twenty people are sprawled across the couches and chairs, all eyes fixed on the pulsing screen. Rani, a beautiful woman who works at the hotel, notices me in the doorway and shouts a welcome. Mahout disengages himself from several companions to shake my hand.

"The great white hunter returns. Come, sit by me and we will talk after the news."

"I'd better go up and shower first."

Looking at his watch, Mahout pats the sofa cushion. "Please, sit. We were not expecting you . . . your room is being used, but not for long."

As I plop down, he asks Rani to speed things up in room thirteen. The evening news, broadcast in Hindi and repeated later in English, is featuring the Indian army. Sri Lanka, once the "Eden of the East," is now a grisly battlefield. Soldiers from the Liberation Tigers of Tamil Eelam have checked the recent advances of Indian troops. Closer to Delhi the Golden Temple, the holiest Sikh shrine, is encircled by soldiers trying to flush out terrorists. The new army contract for the Bofors gun is turning into a national scandal that threatens to topple the ruling party.

Two women saunter in and snuggle up to me on the couch. One purrs, "Are you ready for me?"

Mahout introduces the hotel's newest employees, explaining to them that I'm not a customer but family. Turning to me, he suggests that we dine together in an hour.

As I head up the stairs, Mahout yells, "Hey, wait a second, did you find your duck?"

"Maybe."

I peel off my soiled clothes, which can almost stand on their own, a reminder that my last bath was more than two weeks ago. I stay in the shower until my skin is pulpy; afterward, wanting to look my best, I don my jacket and least wrinkled trousers. The door to Mahout's suite is open.

As I enter, he stops fiddling with his stereo and purses his lips. "Dear me," he sighs, "you must buy some proper clothes."

During the past month, while I was on the trail, Mahout was staying in four star hotels, having traveled literally around the world: Hong Kong, Vancouver, London, Paris, St. Moritz. Business has its rewards, he confides, pouring me a glass of vintage wine. The velvety Bordeaux makes me shiver a bit; only two days ago, dinner meant gruel and tea. He's astonished by my trek in Sikkim. As I might have guessed, the romance of walking with a donkey has never entered his mind.

"Here, try to be civilized," he remarks, handing me a plate of caviar. "You know, I thought of you when I was in Switzerland. There were these Nordic blokes at the hotel insisting that the only time to ski was at night during a full moon."

The sumptuous meal devolves into a small party as other guests join us. Rani is wearing a sari of diaphanous silk and thin silver bracelets that tinkle with every movement. Her toenails are freshly painted, ten cherry half-moons, and gold bands circle her ankles.

I drink far too much, and the next day I awake to a pounding headache. As I stagger through the lobby, Mahout, looking dapper, chirps his salutation.

"What a beautiful day, eh? Where are you going?"

"Ministry of Home Affairs," I growl. "How come you're so sunny? You drank more than I did."

"Here," he says, "take one of these." From a shirt pocket he pulls out a pill the size of a subway token.

"What is it?"

"All I know is that they work," he says with a convincing smile.

The walk perks me up. After my tramp in the hills, strolling these flat city streets seems almost effortless, but I have to force myself to stay alert for speeding motorists, inconsiderate bicyclists, and open manhole covers. I make it to Lok Nayak Bhavan without incident, and the director finds me on the lawn talking to the office workers. He accepts my invitation to lunch as long as we have separate checks. More than ever, I'm glad I avoided offering him baksheesh.

Moments before the food arrives, he conveys the bad news: "The Review Board has denied your request, but . . ." I can bring my case before the minister of home affairs or the prime minister himself; both men have the power to override the Review Board.

"Has that ever happened?" I inquire half-heartedly, pushing my food away.

"Not to my knowledge . . . Can I eat that?" he asks, and thrusts his fork into my fruit. He chats about sports, as India is host of this year's World Cup cricket tournament, and I talk about Gangtok. At the cash register he says, "You know, you really should write a letter to both the minister and the prime minister. You have nothing to lose."

I leave the director and head to Connaught Place, the shopping center of New Delhi. As usual, it is swarming with foreigners buying everything from jeweled baubles to water buffalo burgers. Snake charmers and drug dealers stand next to ice cream vendors; money changers are stationed at every corner; barbers walk along clicking their scissors; professional weighers sit behind scales eyeing fat pedestrians; there are even two men wielding Q-tips, searching for ears to clean. I'm looking for a typewriter shop. I remember seeing one during a previous visit but now can't find it. Policemen are no help, and store owners will talk only about their own wares. Telephone books aren't to be found — they make excellent tinder. I keep walking until at last I spot a young boy carrying a typewriter, and he gives me directions.

The owner of the store explains that his sign crashed to the sidewalk last week. The new sign, he says, "should be ready soon . . . three, four months at the most." I quickly learn that the word "portable" applies to any typewriter that can be lifted by fewer than two people. He has several dozen for rent, and I lease the lightest one, a mere thirty-five-pounder. As I lug it down the street, sweat pours out, and soon my shirt is drenched.

I sit down in my hotel room to compose the letter, summoning the many good reasons why the two most important people in government should intervene on my behalf. After all, I'm looking for the rare pink-headed duck. Page after page curls off the platen, and a numbing sensation of defeat slowly engulfs me. In the end I write a short businesslike letter outlining my search. I hand-deliver the envelopes to the offices and take the long way back to the hotel.

Mahout notices my bleak mood and convinces me to join him for a spin around town. "A ride in a car always helps." We sip two martinis while the vehicle is being readied, and by the time we hit the street I feel much better.

Mahout's car is not what I would have expected; it's an old, dented rust bucket. Behind the wheel is Sanjay, a weight lifter and karate expert. Mahout refers to him as his personal arsenal: "Every part of his body is a lethal weapon." Sanjay opens the door from the inside since the exterior handles are mangled beyond use.

"In my business one should never parade," Mahout advises.

"But I assure you that this car is very special . . . Sanjay will show you what she can do."

The driver nods and opens the throttle, turning loose hundreds of horsepower. It's pedal to the metal, two-wheel turns, and pedestrians be damned. Under the crumpled hood is a customized engine, and I believe Mahout's boast that it can outrun any police car. Sanjay circles India Gate, driving at breakneck speed. The 135-foot stone archway commemorating the 26,000 Indians who died in World War I looms supernaturally large as we careen around it. At this speed, with the tires screeching and the engine howling, we may become its first victims. The two soldiers guarding the eternal flame beneath the arch cheer us on, yelling, "Faster, faster . . . Do it again, faster!"

The next day it's back to my old routine: card games, pots of tea, visits with the director, research in the library, and bird watching around the city. Later in the week the director greets me effusively, saying he has a surprise: the minister has taken a personal interest in my case. He has requested my file and called the director twice.

Mahout is taken aback by the news. "I never thought it would go that far . . . He actually read your letter. What are you going to do?"

There's nothing to do but write yet another letter and wait for a reply. The minister responds favorably, and it's not long before I start visiting his office in North Block. Unlike Lok Nayak Bhavan, North Block is well maintained. This government building and its sister across the street comprise the Secretariat, one of the most imposing sights in New Delhi. The massive complex was built by the British in the early part of the century when New Delhi was chosen to replace Calcutta as the capital. Nearby are the Parliament, the Central Bank, the Archives, the National Museum, and the prime minister's residence, all of which were designed by the British architect Edwin Lutyens, who ignored local sensibilities in favor of Greek and Gothic forms.

Sixteen days after my return from Sikkim, the director calls the Grand Life, leaving a message that doesn't reach me until late in the day. By the time I reach Lok Nayak Bhavan, the director is meeting with someone behind closed doors. The secretary tells me that it may be a long wait. After my second pot of tea I realize that the drink is only making me more jittery.

"I could have told you that," the secretary says. "You are driving me crazy. Please stop pacing . . . Go outside, take a walk."

I chain-smoke as I circle the building. The guard at the front door blocks my reentry.

"New rule," he says. "You have to have the password to get in."

Now I'm really flustered. It's only ten minutes until closing time. The guard whispers the password in my ear.

"Quack."

I force a laugh and rush in to see the director. His door is open and he has good news: the minister has resubmitted my application to the Review Board, recommending a permit. I'm told that the minister has no intention of ruffling feathers by overriding the vote of the Review Board but, as the director says, "His words and recommendation carry weight . . . Things could swing your way." Of course the Review Board will need at least a month to reconsider my application for the Brahmaputra.

"Do you want to wait that long?" the director asks.

With my plan to visit the Gurkhas, a five- or six-week delay would be perfect. Knowing nothing of my intentions, the director issues me another extended pass to the hills.

7

Gurkhaland or Death

THE BUS PULLS into Darjeeling at midmorning on Tuesday, market day. The air is cool and dry, the wind calm. A patchwork of wood and corrugated tin stalls blankets the terraced landscape. Haberdasheries are concentrated at the far end of the market; food stands are grouped in the central area, near the bus stop. Pyramids of mustard, red pepper, curry powder, and saffron blaze in the sunlight. Buddhist shoppers are easy to identify by their maroon robes, as are the Lepchas and the Bhotias in their Tibetan garments of earthen hues, but it's the electric blue and green clothing of the Gurkhas that dominates the scene.

As I wait for my bags to be unloaded, I notice that most of the Ghurka women follow the old tradition of wearing their wealth. Semiprecious stones stud their nostrils, silver bands encircle their arms and ankles, and any gold they own has been hammered into nose rings or set into their teeth. As they talk, and especially when they haggle, they punctuate their words with sudden movements, particularly left-handed jabs and flicks of the wrist. In Gurkha society women are free to curse, smoke, and drink in public.

Chicken feathers still cling to my sweater from the crowded bus ride. As I start to brush them off, the woman who sat next to me rushes over, thinking I'm signaling her. She holds out a bamboo cage full of chickens, asking which one I would like. "No," I say, shaking my head. "No chickens. Only ducks." On the bus she nodded politely when I refused her offer. This time, however, her reaction is quite different. Her brow wrinkles and her black eyes stare into me, searching for another answer. With each second she seems to grow older, her face disintegrating into hatched lines of pain and frustration.

I relent. "I'll take that one," I say, pointing to a small, tired-looking bird. She won't let me have it; it's not good enough for me. The people clustered around us agree with her choice of a plumper, feistier bird. After we conclude the deal, everyone seems amused, especially the seller, who has miraculously regained her youth. As usual, I'm the last to realize how ridiculous I look holding the chicken by its spindly legs. When I smile the crowd starts to laugh. The noise attracts more people. A barber comes out of his shop with a half-shaven customer behind him. For a brief moment business around the bus stop comes to a halt while everyone investigates the commotion. I wobble along, my suitcases in one hand, the chicken in the other. Progress is slow and awkward. Two youngsters dart to my side, offering to carry my bags.

"How much?" I ask.

They look at me askance. Someone in the crowd speaks up: "This is not Calcutta. There is no charge." I apologize to the boys, who bob their heads and grab my bags. They're wearing canvas shorts and gaily colored caps with a tuck at the peak. Their sockless feet make squishing sounds inside their rubber shoes as they lead me toward a set of wide steps connecting the market to Landella Road, the main street of Darjeeling. Shawls and woolen goods for sale are displayed on the handrails. With winter coming, business is brisk, and the stairway is crowded with buyers. As we reach the first landing, I hear a loud voice: "Welcome to Darjeeling. We received your telegram."

I can't see who's talking. In Nepalese I reply, "Hello."
There's no response. It must be someone from the GNLF. As
M.M. had instructed, I had sent my contact a telegram with my
itinerary.

"Hello," I repeat.

The boys point up the stairs. The people draw back, forming a corridor to the uppermost landing, about thirty feet
above. A platoon of men stand there, motionless, the sun at
their backs silhouetting them. I climb slowly, pausing on each
tread. The chicken squawks from the pressure I unconsciously
exert on its legs. Nervously I squint upward. One step from
the landing, I reach out for the hand of the tallest man. For
a Gurkha he's a giant, almost my size. All six of the men wear
kukris, the curved knives that are the trademark of the Gurkha
warrior.

I shake hands with the entire welcoming committee and
turn to face the market. In the process of turning, I snag my
pants on the tip of the big man's kukri. As I try to free the knife
from my belt loop, the chicken pecks viciously at the man's
thigh. The warrior glares at me, but the crowd loves it.

Free of the knife, I triumphantly raise the chicken into the
air and acknowledge the people jostling for a clear view. The
boys stick close by, not sure whether to drop the bags and run
or stand proud. Luckily, they stay put.

The large man raises his hands, quieting the onlookers. The
soldiers on either side of me step forward to the edge of the
stone landing, then draw their kukris in a synchronized motion. The polished blades glint in the sunlight. Loudly and
clearly, they proclaim, "Long live Gurkhaland . . . Gurkhaland
or death!"

Over and over they repeat the slogan. I study the faces of
the people below me, captivated by the sudden change in their
expressions. "Gurkhaland or death! Gurkhaland or death!"
The words excite the crowd. Smiles become scowls as
clenched fists punch the air. Men and women, young and old,

pick up the chant. More kukris are unsheathed and waved as voices cry out for Gurkhaland.

Once more the big man holds his hands up, but this time it takes a moment to reclaim the silence. He walks down several steps and turns to face the western horizon. Taking a deep breath, he trumpets: "Long live Subash Ghising! Long live our divine leader Subash Ghising!" The hillside erupts, picking up the new chant. Not waiting for the noise to subside, my hosts lead me up the steps. The chanting follows us down the street and into the lobby of a dilapidated three-story rooming house. The proprietor quakes in the presence of the GNLF.

"He will provide whatever you need," the big man says to me in a commanding voice. "Headquarters will send for you tomorrow, OK?"

I thank them and ask their names. The leader comes to attention, saying, "We are soldiers fighting for Gurkhaland."

"Of course," I say, taking a step back.

The troops leave and the chanting subsides. Before going up to my room, I hire the boys to tend my chicken. They promise to protect it with their lives. When I ask them what grade they are in, R. P. Pradhan, the oldest boy, tells me that neither of them has been in school for three years. Like their unemployed fathers, they spend their days looking for odd jobs to put food on the family table.

"I stay away from home until I get money," R.P. says. "Me, too," adds his pal, also named Pradhan.

As I soon learn, being out of work in Darjeeling is the rule, not the exception. Unemployment statistics are no longer published. As one social worker tells me later, "Everyone knows the bad news. Why post it and make it worse?"

My room is furnished with a cot, a chair, and a sink. Hanging on a hook next to the door is a key to the hallway toilet, a closet with a porcelain hole in the floor. Two windows look out on the courtyard of an adjacent tenement. I watch an elderly woman cradling a baby near the entrance. She's sitting in a chair, rocking gently back and forth. A kukri lies at her feet.

The manager brings in a desk, and I sit there and think for the next hour. When I was in Sikkim, my friend M.M. often talked about the Gurkha cause, describing it romantically. "When you have been chained for years, a gun becomes your best friend. You never want to be chained again . . . Revolt liberates everything inside you."

When I discussed this with Padam, he concurred, noting that the struggle for freedom was bigger than any of my dreams. "Face it," he told me, "when you sight down the barrel of a gun, you see things nobody else can see."

During the raj the British called Darjeeling "the queen of the hill stations." It had the best colonial hospitals and was the ideal spot to recuperate from the debilitating heat and diseases found in southern India. At the turn of the century, and continuing well into the 1950s, Darjeeling was the choicest of Indian resorts. The governor-general summered here, as well as the top echelon of the army and the wealthy of Calcutta. In 1909 there was a six-year waiting list for membership in the exclusive Tea Planters' Club, renamed the Gymkhana Club after independence.

At present the streets of Darjeeling are crumbling, the hospital understaffed, the electricity off as often as it's on. Unlike Gangtok, where it's hard to escape the noise of heavy equipment, there appears to be little new construction. The buildings downtown all need painting. Shop windows display faded goods next to dusty sale signs. Merchants along Landella Road spend much of the day sitting on chairs outside their shops. The owner of an antiques store tells me that business has been bad for almost two years, ever since the fighting started.

The surroundings, however, are idyllic. To the north the

mountains of Sikkim tower above the clouds; to the west, far in the distance, Mount Everest rules the horizon; to the east the Rangeet River shimmers like a ribbon of silver. On sunny days the Chowrasta, an open square at the foot of Observatory Hill, is crowded with people. At least fifteen mules or donkeys are usually hitched to the base of its large fountain. It's an excellent place to launch a kite, and whenever school is out, the sky is alive with paper birds. On top of the hill a shrine marks the former home of the fabled mystic Dor-jey, for whom the town is named. Although the Chowrasta area has always been a holy place to Buddhists and Hindus, only the British were allowed near the square during the raj. Jawans, the local police, used lengths of hose to chase away any nonwhite. Now streams of people visit the temple each day. As they leave, the faithful ring the bell above the entryway, hoping their prayers will ride heavenward on the sound.

On either side of the square is a path that rims the hill and connects the town with the Tibetan Refugee Center, founded in 1959 and now home to several hundred followers of the Dalai Lama. The Tibetan elders resolutely look forward to the next life, having abandoned hope of returning to a free Tibet. The children, scarred by a life of exile and poverty, tell me that they will fight the Chinese when they are older. No doubt they will be the soldiers in Sonam's army.

A mile beyond the refugee center is the Darjeeling zoo, a depressing place. A snow leopard paces the cement floor and butts its head against a chain-link fence; the Bengal tigers paw tight cages. Not far from the zoo is the Indian Mountaineering Institute, which is dedicated to Tenzing Norkay, the first man to climb Mount Everest. More than half the floor space is given over to displays of equipment used on various expeditions. It's hard to sustain interest in exhibit after exhibit of moth-eaten parkas and old boots.

In the small observatory detached from the main building is a large Zeiss telescope, which I use to scan the area for birds.

Numerous crested buntings, plovers, and paradise flycatchers swoop by. Off to the east a blue-winged teal dabs in a rock pool near the river. This encourages me, for the teal's diet and habitat are the same as those of the pink-headed duck. As I'm leaving, I notice a plaque on the wall. The telescope was a present to an Indian prince from Adolf Hitler.

Until I have time to investigate the rock pool and the small lakes in the region, I roam the market. Unfortunately, the poultry dealers only scratch their heads when I exhibit the picture of the missing bird. No one has seen or heard of it.

"Does anyone hunt anymore?" I ask one fowl vendor, hoping to hook up with one of the guides who serviced the English hunting parties in the early 1960s.

"Hunt?" the man asks. "Not for sport. Not anymore. We are in the middle of a war."

"Are any of the old guides around?"

"They are soldiers now. Go to the GNLF."

The next day, as I leave the Tibet Restaurant after breakfast, a man whistles to me. When I approach, he whispers, "Headquarters has sent me."

We follow a narrow footpath through back yards, gardens, and goat pens reminiscent of those in a terraced Italian village. Laundry dries in the breeze, and the smell of garlic floats through the air. Women lean out of windows on crossed arms watching children kick a soccer ball. As we come around a hairpin turn, I confront a giant portrait of a man painted on the side of a boulder. It's Subash Ghising, president and founder of the Gurkha National Liberation Front; I can't determine whether he's smiling or sneering.

Along the base of the mural is the flag of Gurkhaland. I'm later told that Ghising worked closely with astrologers on its design. In this hill culture the occult frequently controls people's lives. The GNLF relies on astrologers to forecast the most auspicious days on which to schedule meetings, strikes, and even gun battles.

"Everything has meaning," my escort informs me. "Signs ride on the wind."

Just beyond the tip of Ghising's tie, the path veers to the right, and there's another mural. This one shows a map of the proposed Gurkhaland, a 2,500-square-mile tract with a population of a million people, 70 percent of whom are Gurkhas. This ideal Gurkha state is bounded by Nepal on the west and Assam to the east; Siliguri marks the southern extreme, while Sikkim and Bhutan form the northern frontier.

Ironically, the GNLF headquarters is one of the few buildings in the neighborhood not covered with political graffiti. It's a simple two-story concrete house that Ghising bought years ago. He still uses a couple of rooms above the offices as an apartment. A dozen men mill about the entrance with their kukris ever ready. I offer my camera bag to one of them for inspection. He ignores it and orders me to wait.

A shrill whistle cuts the air. I trace it to a sentry on a rooftop. Other lookouts are posted atop cars, porches, and rock ledges. Each of them signals all clear.

"Now you can go in."

I walk across the concrete porch and stop in the mud room, my progress blocked by the largest man I've seen in the hills. "Welcome," he bellows, extending his hand and introducing himself as C. P. Chetri. He leads me down a corridor, nodding at the three men guarding a door. They relax their grip on their kukris.

I follow him into a tiny office with two chairs, a desk, and an old typewriter. A kukri hangs from a nail in the stucco wall. Three frayed extension cords hang from a light fixture and run down a corner of the room. Nothing is plugged into them.

After ten minutes the president calls for me. I enter a room filled with fourteen men and three women. They introduce themselves, each mentioning his or her title as a member of the GNLF Central Council. Two unshaded bulbs light the room. Ghising sits at one end of a long row of metal chairs, looking exactly like his portrait. The very first Gurkhaland flag is tacked above his head. As I inspect it, one of the council members explains its symbols.

The green field represents land and self-determination. Three stars denote the union of Nepalese, Bhotia, and Lepcha ethnic groups into the Gurkha cause. The stars' four points signify the marriage of the three groups with destiny, a future that only the GNLF can deliver. Four horizontal bars on the bottom stand for opportunity, equality, fraternity, and liberty. The kukri, with its curved tip pointing to the uppermost star, evokes the Gurkhas' history as the warriors of the Himalayas.

I'm directed to a seat opposite Ghising. He's wearing a down jacket, a white shirt, and a striped tie. His twill pants are rolled above his ankles, and he constantly slips his feet in and out of his black shoes. Every couple of minutes he checks his cap, adjusting the angle ever so slightly.

Eighteen cups of steaming tea are brought into the cold room. Ghising makes sure that I'm served first. The tea is a special blend of golden blossoms and first-flush leaves, a present from the pickers at a famous estate. The president and I stare at each other, neither of us saying a word, moving as mirror images, raising our cups at the same time, crossing our legs simultaneously.

Unsure of protocol, I begin by complimenting the tea. My remark sparks a ten-minute review of the harvest. During the discussion the hierarchy of the council emerges. However, the moment Ghising holds forth, everyone else hushes, no one daring to interrupt him. His English is better than I had expected and rarely does he need the interpreter. After an hour it's apparent that the GNLF is a one-man show. If I'm to understand the Gurkha dream of freedom, I must understand Ghising. I ask him for a private interview. He agrees to talk, but not in private.

"Start now, if you like," he says.

I take out a notebook and a tape recorder. He shakes his

head and waves a finger at the machine. "No taping. I will speak slowly for you."

And so begins the first of many conversations.

Subash Ghising claims to have come into life unaided, already suckling when the midwife arrived at the Mon Ju tea estate in 1936. One of eight children, he left school after the ninth grade to help his father, the estate superintendent. Unlike most Gurkha families, they had adequate food and clothing.

In 1953, at the age of seventeen, he enlisted in the Eighth Gurkha Regiment of the Indian Army. He blossomed in the military, resuming his education and developing skills as an artist and writer. He also trained in the gymnasium and became the bantam-weight boxing champ of his regiment. He says he can't remember losing a fight.

"I am a winner," he tells me again and again.

During his third year in the army, Ghising's life changed radically. He was stationed in the Naga Hills as part of a massive federal campaign to suppress rebellious tribal groups fighting against what they considered the tyranny of the men from the plains.

"I was in the jungle," he recalls. "I killed many men. Most I shot, others I attacked with my kukri. One day a noise, probably a branch breaking, made me look up. I found myself staring into the eyes of a Naga. My gun jammed . . . I reached for my kukri. I was about to kill him when he cried out in Nepalese: 'Why are you killing us? We are only fighting for our land, for our rights as Indians.' It was as if Shiva was speaking to me, and I never killed again." As he speaks, Ghising acts out his story, pretending the room is the rain forest and a chair the Naga.

His epiphany in the jungle ended his career as a soldier. Several months later he entered college in Darjeeling to study political theory and writing. By the time he was thirty, he had completed twenty novels, each a romance story with a happy ending. (I found it impossible to secure a copy of anything he had written.)

While teaching kindergarten to pay the rent, Ghising became active in local politics. He proudly tells me that he led the first violent demonstration in Darjeeling history. His hands rip the air as he enacts the rock-throwing incident. The issue at the time (and one that still exists) was Calcutta's insistence on filling vacancies in the region's bureaucracy with people from Calcutta, not Darjeeling. Interestingly, Ghising was the only one of twenty-three demonstrators not sentenced to a lengthy prison term. No one testified against him.

"I was and am a strong man," he cautions.

He remained active in radical politics until he joined a group of businessmen and retired army officers to found the Gurkha National Liberation Front in 1980. This alliance between a man on the fringe and the middle class of Darjeeling seemed natural at the time. Ghising had a reputation for action, they had the money, and everyone agreed that Gurkha rights were being trampled.

Darjeeling's long, steady decline began when the British left and the district was absorbed by West Bengal. The courts and many government offices were relocated to Calcutta, the state capital. Darjeeling, formerly given special treatment, suddenly lost much of its government funding. Because of its then prosperous tea and logging industries, the resort town was able to postpone the effects of neglect until the mid-1970s. But then the infrastructure started to fall apart: municipal services were curtailed, water pipes burst, roads caved in, sewers collapsed. Ghising promised his backers that he could turn things around.

Few people rallied to his cause, and the GNLF remained a small, rather ineffective organization for more than six years. There were no demonstrations and not one arrest during this time. The man of action was stalled. Some said he was following the orders of the middle-class Gurkhas funding the GNLF.

When I mention this, Ghising jumps up from his chair and approaches me. "I was educating the people. That is a long, slow process . . . Whoever told you that lied."

No one disputes that in 1986 life changed for Ghising, the GNLF, and every Gurkha in India. "It was amazing," Ghising remarks in a cooler voice. "It all happened so quickly."

Hundreds of miles away, in the northeastern state of Meghalaya, the resident Gurkhas were expelled. State leaders, sure that outsiders were depriving natives of jobs, decided that deporting all nonnatives was the best way to protect the state's heritage and culture. They backed the xenophobic cry sweeping the area: "Meghalaya for Meghalayans." Gurkhas were singled out because in earlier years Gurkha troops had gunned down tribal insurgents. Almost all the displaced Gurkhas landed in Darjeeling, where they had relatives. The refugees' stories fueled anger and paranoia. Many Gurkhas wondered about the status of their rights as Indian citizens. The incidents in Meghalaya suggested that all Nepalese-speaking Indians would be treated as foreigners.

At last Ghising had found his springboard. After working day and night for a week, he announced a plan that would ensure the property and rights of every Gurkha. A demonstration was organized and 3,500 people gathered to hear him speak.

"As I walked to the podium, I knew my destiny was being revealed," Ghising recalls.

Waving a kukri over his head, Ghising made the speech of a lifetime. With a sweep of the blade, he severed ties with his middle-class backers. He proclaimed the GNLF as "the party of the people . . . the party of action." He issued a formal demand for the creation of Gurkhaland. It would be, he promised the cheering throng, a part of India, but first and foremost it would be their homeland.

"Gurkhaland is dearer than life," he said over and over in his speech, launching the party's first slogan.

By all accounts Ghising was brilliant that night. His language was tough, his politics radical, and the people loved it. As one eyewitness told me, "He freed everything inside us."

The speech catapulted Ghising and the GNLF into prominence. He galvanized a proud warrior culture with words threatening violence and promising freedom. Monthly party meetings became weekly and then nightly affairs. Military training camps were opened, a youth wing was formed, and local party chapters were established around the countryside. Darjeeling, a small mountain town, thus began its militant campaign against Calcutta, the lowland giant.

8

Mountains of Trouble

COME DARK, Darjeeling shutters up. The only people on the street are tourists in thick-soled hiking boots. I slip into one of the few restaurants open after sunset and take a corner table. In the middle of the room a party of boisterous Germans make toasts and drain their beers. Groups of French, Spanish, and Italian trekkers speak in low voices or study their tea. I recognize my waiter from the GNLF headquarters, where he often stands guard during the day. He brings over a candle when he sees me writing. I ask him why the town closes so early.

"The night belongs to the state police . . . Patrols are everywhere," he says, pulling up a chair, his eyes on my scribbling.

When he takes my order, he warns me that my choice of vegetables and rice is all wrong. He recommends a hamburger or pizza, the house specialties, but my order stands. As he goes to the kitchen, he flips on the stereo. Seconds later the Grateful Dead booms from the speakers. The other foreigners start to tap their feet and sing along. Behind the counter the chef weaves and bobs while he slices. The owner raps the cash box, using his pencil as a drumstick. Briefly, the idea of appointing rock stars as ambassadors makes sense.

"Keep on truckin'," the waiter calls after I finish eating and head out the door.

It's a beautiful night, and the Milky Way, a faint silver brush-stroke, lures me to the Chowrasta. There's no one about, just a night heron stalking the fountain for insects. Shooting stars flash across the sky. I sit on a bench and imagine myself a dupchen sailing along an astral stream through the heavens. The earth fades to a dot of blue light on my horizon.

"Hands on your head," a voice commands in Hindi, abruptly ending my voyage. Flashlights snap on. I raise my hands. Eight soldiers fan out. The two in the middle approach as the others train rifles on me. An officer searches my bag, finds nothing, and demands to see my papers. My passport is in my pocket. May I lower my hands? He nods and advises me not to make a sudden move. Once the safety catches click on, most of the tension eases. I hand over my documents, trying to explain why I'm in the Chowrasta. He grunts and orders me to return to my hotel.

The next day at least five people ask me about the incident in the Chowrasta. Because so few people have telephones, the GNLF has developed a finely tuned grapevine.

There's an unexpected benefit of my meeting with the state police. I'm invited by a GNLF lieutenant, T. P. Chetri, to accompany him to Tiger Hill, a promontory eleven miles out of town, the next day to watch "the most beautiful thing in the world." He's referring to daybreak in the Himalayas.

T.P. drives his Land Rover as if he's rushing an accident victim to the hospital. According to the almanac, dawn at sea level is around six, but it's almost forty minutes later when the first light hits Darjeeling; it's a long climb over the tip of the Himalayas. A sublime piece of that solar arc awaits the early morning visitor to Tiger Hill. T.P. stands close to me at the overlook. Only a few cumulus clouds drift overhead, great puffs of white smoke. The view is uninterrupted for hundreds of miles. I can see the mountains of Nepal, Tibet, and Bhutan. As the sky lightens to a powder blue, he extends his arm and moves it slowly left to right.

"Look at it," he exclaims. "Such beauty. This is what our fight is about. This is our home. This is Gurkhaland . . . I want my children to come here. I have no money, but I can give them this."

T.P. joined the GNLF a week after Ghising's momentous speech and has been actively involved in the struggle ever since. As we drive back, I wonder how the GNLF will be able to secure his legacy. Conspicuously absent from the party platform is any mention of Gurkhaland's future government; this doesn't seem to bother anyone but me. It's unthinkable to T.P. that things won't work out like the happy endings in Ghising's novels.

"When my mail is addressed Gurkhaland, India, everything we want to happen will happen. Mister Ghising will guide us."

The West Bengal state government is controlled by the Marxist Left Front party. Jyoti Basu, chief minister and party leader, is firmly entrenched, having been in power for more than fifteen years. Initially he ignored the GNLF's demands, keeping his energy and treasury focused on Calcutta, where the needs were most pressing. Several months after Ghising rallied the people, the GNLF backed up their rhetoric with violence, torching state buildings in the hill district.

"We had to send a message to Basu," T.P. explains. "We said we would fight, and we meant it."

Basu was enraged by the violence and dispatched troops to restore order. He labeled Ghising a rebel and the GNLF a bunch of criminals. The arrival of the state troops, commonly known as the CRPF (Central Reserve Police Force), only heightened the tension. Reluctant to shoot at the local police, many of whom are party members, the GNLF started to terrorize the soldiers from Calcutta. Barracks were bombed and roads booby-trapped.

"It all led up to Kalimpong," T.P. informs me. "That is when we became an army and started fighting fire with fire."

On a date picked by GNLF astrologers, July 27, 1986, Ghising scheduled a mass demonstration in Kalimpong, the second largest city in the district. Busloads of Gurkhas poured into the town, and the police, unnerved by the swelling crowd, suddenly declared the assembly illegal, ordering the 40,000 Gurkhas to disperse. No one left.

A group of college students began taunting the CRPF. A rock was thrown, and the poorly trained soldiers rushed the students, thrashing them with bamboo sticks. The crowd started marching and chanting slogans, but when they reached the police barricades and refused to stop, the troops opened fire. Three girls, all under seventeen, were shot. The marchers regrouped, and this time the police shot twenty-five Gurkhas. Kukris came out, and several CRPF officers were killed, one beheaded by a Gurkha grandmother; with two whacks of a blade, she avenged the death of her granddaughter.

From this incident an elite paramilitary unit called the Gurkha Volunteer Cell (GVC) was organized by former commandos in the Indian and British armies. Rigorously trained, the volunteers were shaped into a deadly army.

By now I know most of the guards by name at the GNLF headquarters. Ghising and I have been meeting for almost a week and there's little time before the next Gurkha demonstration, the first in many months. Party officials expect a turnout of 500,000 supporters.

"It is a call to arms," Ghising warns. "We must take charge again. The peace talks were nothing but garbage."

A cease-fire has been in effect since the summer, when Ghising went to New Delhi for peace talks mediated by the federal government. The demand for Gurkhaland was flatly rejected, and Ghising was urged to accept a generously funded Hill Council, which would be a relatively autonomous governing body with locally elected representatives. Ghising rejected the compromise, and the upcoming demonstration is to be a show of defiance: copies of the government proposal will be handed out and burned.

"After the rally," Ghising vows, pulling his chair next to mine, and speaking in a low, intense voice, "we will close the district. A general strike will shut down everything . . . We will strike until Gurkhaland is ours."

He has placed all GVC units on alert. "I promise you," he says, "that there will be no stopping us once we start fighting again." Inspired by his own words, he's suddenly on his feet, shaking a fist. "We mean business . . . These politicians treat us like animals in the zoo, but we will fight like tigers. We will win!"

"There's no chance for peace?" I ask.

"We are Gurkhas! We are born fighters!"

The next morning I learn that Ghising likes me even though he doesn't agree with me on most issues. Appointments are no longer necessary; I can come and go as I please. He even offers me the limited use of a car and a driver.

"Let's go to a tea estate," I suggest to the driver, R. R. Pradhan, a former British commando wearing two kukris. He rounds up a couple of GVC soldiers to accompany us. An hour later we're waist deep in a sea of tea bushes. As far as the eye can see, there are neat rows of identical bushes, all between three and four feet high. In the distance tea pickers hunch over the crop, pinching leaves and dropping them into wicker baskets. The oblong leaves are tough and leathery, their appearance giving no hint of the tender flavor within.

Tea is the lifeblood of the GNLF and Darjeeling. It's by far the area's largest industry, employing 50,000 full-time workers and many more part time. For the past four decades the harvest has consistently yielded twelve to fourteen million kilos. In 1985 total revenues were $40 million, but few of the estates are profitable; most of them are referred to as "sick gardens," one step ahead of bank foreclosure.

"The tea industry is a mess. Big trouble," R. R. Pradhan tells me before slipping into a cockney accent, peppering his language with army slang. "Gawd awful . . . The state took over a lot of the gardens when the Brits left and started buggering the people. Calcutta, those berks . . ."

Most of the gardens, I learn, are more than a hundred years old and are still planted with original stock. Bushes grown from seed will produce high yields for only sixty or seventy years, while clonal bushes are productive for half that time. Replanting and experiments in hybridization, though not totally abandoned, were cut from estate budgets after 1947. As a result, many nurseries have become jungles of weeds, and few new strains have been introduced.

I'm inspecting the contorted lower branches and root system of a bush when I hear my name being called. Someone is sprinting toward me, running down the narrow chute between two rows of bushes. B.B., my self-appointed host, invites me to join him for a cup of tea. We walk to a small house he shares with seven other workers. Half the roof is thatch, the rest is corrugated tin and plywood. Lengths of bamboo have been lashed together and fashioned into a gutter.

B.B. picks up the hingeless door and moves it to the side so we can enter the house. Posters of American pop stars cover the cracked mud walls. A paneless window looks to the northwest, framing a postcard view of the Sikkimese mountains. Several chickens follow us inside to scratch the dirt floor. In the main room a plywood sheet on some tea crates serves as a table. A cook stove has been built from loose stones, and next to it is the kitchen sink, a red plastic bucket. While B.B. stokes the fire, I look into the bedroom, where eight slabs of foam stretch across more tea crates. Family photos and images ripped from magazines are tacked above each pillow. B.B. shows me his area. It's the one with the pictures of palm trees and south sea islands.

"I wanted to join the navy, but I am a Gurkha so they made

me enlist in the army," he complains as the tea kettle begins hissing.

He lifts up his mattress and pulls out a crate. Inside there's a radio, a silver bracelet, some money, and a few odds and ends he won't let me see. Next to his kukri, these are his most valuable possessions. He shows me a picture of his parents holding him as a baby. I concur that his mother was beautiful and that his father looked very strong.

"He gave me this," B.B. says proudly, brandishing the largest kukri I've ever seen. It looks more like a scimitar than a knife. While I examine the polished, razor-sharp blade, he announces he will die before being separated from it.

We return to the main room, and B.B. serves the tea, which is better than that served at party headquarters. He perks up when I tell him this and discloses his secret for a perfect blend. Most of his instructions are lost on me, as they require an intimate knowledge of the estate. Slope and exposure are important: the more southern the exposure and the steeper the hill, the better the tea. Leaves grown on the north side of a hill yield an acidic, tangy taste, and B.B. adds a small amount of them for zing.

He tells me that like every other tea garden in the Darjeeling district, this is a GNLF bastion: everyone belongs to the party. Two teams of GVC soldiers, armed for battle, patrol the grounds at all times. B.B. shows me his set of fatigues. When he dons them, he's no longer a tea garden worker, but a man with great purpose, a freedom fighter. "I feel strong when I am on patrol. I can kill hundreds of the CRPF."

Voices outside the door announce the arrival of a large group of men. Another pot of tea is prepared and cups are brought in from the other houses. We squat, our backs pressed against the walls. My notebook is open on my knees. The leader of the GVC brigade watches me write as the others talk. After a minute or so he rushes toward me, demanding to see the book. I refuse.

"What did he tell you?" he snaps, pointing at B.B.

I assure him that B.B. spoke in glowing terms about the GNLF and Subash Ghising.

"Ha! I am the most loyal follower of Mister Ghising," he dictates. "Write that down."

Another man, shorter than the rest, proclaims that he's the most dedicated. Soon the house is filled with shouting men fiercely professing their allegiance to the GNLF. The leader stands. As he speaks, his body stiffens, muscles flexing, but his voice is soft.

"Pledge yourselves to Mister Ghising, our divine leader."

The men gather around him, grabbing their kukris, and slide the blades across their forefingers. The chickens rush to peck at the dark splotches on the dirt floor as the men scrawl in blood across one wall "Gurkhaland or death."

It's late afternoon when we head back to Darjeeling. The sun is fading, but with distance, the events of the day are becoming even more vivid in my mind. I now better understand how Ghising sees himself as a fighting messiah, a leader inspired by heaven and endowed by its divine powers. "I am everything in all ways," he once said to me. "No one can tell me what to do or how to do it." The Gurkhas, taught since birth to revere the Hindu pantheon of warrior-gods, have accorded him this role, and they seem to applaud his every move.

The next day I enlist R. R. Pradhan and his car in my search for the pink-headed duck. My walks have been disappointing from a bird watcher's point of view, and I want to investigate some marshes outside of town. My companion listens politely to my tales about the duck, but from the way he fidgets and glances about, it's obvious that he isn't interested.

"Birds," he tells me later, "are good in a stew, but I really like them roasted over a fire."

The only duck I've seen around Darjeeling is the teal I

spotted through the telescope at the Mountaineering Institute. Again today, not a duck in sight. In the first wetlands we visit we find a couple of black partridges and a flock of little stints. At another marsh, closer to the Rangeet River, I spot an Indian skimmer, a bird that flies an inch or two above the surface while dragging the tip of its lower mandible through the water. I would be happy to sit and study it for hours, but R.R. gets restless after a few minutes and starts hacking a path through the bamboo to the water's edge.

"Reminds me of Borneo," he says between strokes of his machete. "It was hotter there, but the bamboo was like this. I remember a time . ." and he launches into a war story from his days as a British Gurkha.

The skimmer is gone by the time we reach the water. We have to wait thirty minutes before another bird appears, a pied cuckoo, which lands for a drink. R.R. fires a stone at it, sending it racing for cover inside the montane jungle.

"Habit," he says defensively. "I can't help it."

We hike back to the car and drive to town. Along the way we pass teams of men unloading trucks filled with coils of barbed wire, sheets of plywood with broken bottles glued on one side, logs, and steel I-beams. R.R. waves to each work party, promising to return once he drops me off.

"We have learned a thing or two from our other blockades," R.R. says. "This time we will seal off every road and do it right."

Today, November 17, less than a week from the start of the blockade and general strike, the market is busier than ever as Gurkhas begin warehousing supplies. The lines for rice, flour, potatos, and radishes are long. There is no more sugar, and merchants are taking orders for a shipment due soon. The average Gurkha can barely feed his family as things are now, but people are lively, most of them smiling. What will they eat if the strike lasts beyond a week?

"We will manage," one person tells me. Another says,

"Ram will protect us," sentiments echoed by everyone I ask.

Ghising points out that life in the hills has never been easy, but that Gurkhas view hardship and suffering as separate conditions. Hardship is part of everyday life, and it merely intensifies during a strike. Going to bed with a half-filled stomach is life as it is. Suffering, on the other hand, is something provoked by external forces: Calcutta and its oppression cause suffering.

The mood at party headquarters grows more militant as the strike nears. Sentries no longer pitch coins or shuffle about. Everyone is on alert. Ghising's language changes as well. He begins using verbs like "attack," "strangle," "retaliate," and "bomb." He speaks with the confidence of a general in charge of a well-equipped army, but he tells me that the GNLF has neither automatic weapons nor grenade launchers. Although state investigators have found no evidence of Chinese or Nepalese arms shipments to the GNLF, rumors persist, alleging that the Gurkhas have a very sophisticated arsenal.

"At last count," Ghising reveals, "we had twenty thousand rifles. We have many more bombs. Everything is handmade . . . Gurkhas are smart, not rich."

He invites me to inspect various GNLF armories, and the next day I depart on a tour with R.R. and two GVC officers. We drive eastward toward Lankapara Hat. My visa isn't valid for travel in this area, but the GVC troops refuse to conceal me. To take such a precaution would be demeaning. On the first two days of our trip we visit three rather sleepy tea estates, none of which is well equipped. During the morning of the third day, before we head away from the Bhutanese border, I decide to go for a walk while the others have tea. With the frontier less than a mile from the safe house where we've been sleeping, I'm determined to put at least one foot inside Bhutan. Across the border I let out my pink-headed duck call. It has been a while since I last tried it, and I'm a bit rusty. I try again. As I'm about to issue another call, I hear a crackle

The last reliable sighting of the pink-headed duck
(Rhodonessa caryophyllacea) occurred in 1935.

During the raj a few pink-headed ducks turned up each year in the open markets of Gangtok, Sikkim.

There is always room for one more on the bus to Sikkim.

A road worker in Sikkim pounds rocks into gravel. This has been her job for thirty years.

This shopkeeper in Gangtok had never heard of the fabled duck.

High above the Tista River near the giant rhododendron forest, reputed home of Me-Gu, the Abominable Snowman.

The intrepid boys who tended my chicken in Darjeeling.

Subash Ghising, revered leader of the Gurkha National Liberation Front.

Tea plantation workers of Darjeeling.

Gurkha guerrillas with typical homemade weapons put together from water pipe, bits of old cars, wire, and twine.

Shankar and I met by chance in New Delhi and teamed up for the river voyage through Assam.

I prepare *Lahey-Lahey* for our journey down the Brahmaputra, likely home of the pink-headed duck.

Our palace on the river bank south of Tezpur.

Left: A Brahmaputra freighter being pulled off a shoal. *Right:* A boatload of thatch being taken to market near Sibsagar. *Below:* Fishermen along the river believe whirlpools are gateways to another world. We almost found out for ourselves in a whirlpool much bigger than this.

The woeful crew of the fishing boat *Lucky*, a name the skipper, Gopal, is ready to change.

In dacoit-infested waters, boats form convoys and anchor together at night.

Fishermen like these from Jorhat often laze under their nets during the day. They fish only at night, using lamps as lures.

Our favorite tea shop near Majuli, the world's largest river island.

Mukhya, leader of the Aunia Ati Satra, a commune on Majuli, is said to have the power of the third eye.

Prem, my guide to the Tantric way, at Kamakhya Temple.

. . . something running from me? . . . No, it's moving toward me. The sounds are getting louder. A moment later my companions are yelling at me, making me promise not to leave their sight again.

Just before noon we stop to inspect what I'm told is a very militant tea garden. We conceal the jeep in a stand of bamboo and ascend a path leading to a grassy field used as a commons by the 168 Gurkhas living on the estate. The leader agrees to muster his troops, sending two aides into the fields and excusing himself to retrieve his own weapon. His rifle is beautiful, a work of art, embellished with intricate silver scrollwork and a circular pattern of kukris.

"I made it myself," he says, stroking the barrel.

We follow him to the back of his house, where a Belgian shotgun is lying across two sawhorses. It was left by the former owner of the estate and is now used as a model by teenagers making their first guns. I'm shown other works in progress and discover new uses for old automobile parts. The roof supports from early Land Rovers make excellent gun barrels, better than the lengths of water pipe that are also used. Pieces of carburetors can be filed into firing pins and trigger mechanisms; parts from the choke system can be transformed into gun sights; bits from the starter motor find new life as shell extractors.

A public address system shatters the calm, blaring a call to arms as a World War II air raid siren wails. The workers in the field drop their baskets and run for weapons hidden in tunnels dug throughout the estate. I watch one woman raise a trap door concealed by brambles and dirt. She vanishes down the hole and comes up clutching a rifle. Within minutes everyone is in formation, awaiting orders. During all this, the leader has had his eyes on his watch.

"Not good enough," he scolds his troops, parading in front of them.

One by one, the army of men and women, young and old,

present their arms; those who don't have rifles show me their kukris. Many of the guns appear more likely to damage the shooter than the target. A demonstration is held to prove reliability and accuracy. The test is impressive: no one misses the target on the barn, nearly one hundred yards away. But the guns are heavy and awkward, no match for those of the state police.

"Now we will show you our secret weapons," the leader says, tipping his head toward four men, who dash off. They return carrying a crossbow and what appears to be several large balls of twine. Under each ball of jute, however, is a piece of lead pipe filled with black powder and an assortment of nails, ball bearings, shards of glass, and metal scrap. The crossbow is nicknamed "the Silencer." According to the marksman holding it, the ancient weapon is still the most effective way to take out a sentry. As I reach for one of the arrows, he cautions me: the tips have been dipped in poison. A short prayer to Kali, imploring the goddess of destruction to guide the arrow, is painted along the hardwood shaft.

The leader takes one of the bombs and tosses it like a softball to a man twenty yards away. The Gurkha waves us behind him. He kisses the stubby two-inch fuse and lights it, holding the bomb for several agonizing seconds before heaving it behind the barn. The explosion is followed by an eerie shriek as shrapnel whizzes through the air. The crowd cheers and starts chanting, "Gurkhaland, Gurkhaland . . ."

After three days near the frontier, I return to Darjeeling to find the GNLF headquarters jammed with people. It's November 21, the eve of the demonstration. I assume the final details are being worked out, but a friend tells me I'm wrong: the rally has been postponed and the strike canceled. Ghising is leaving today to resume negotiations in New Delhi.

Having accepted an invitation from the federal government, Ghising is a changed man. Gone is the fiery talk; his mood and tone are conciliatory, but he refuses to explain his decision, saying only, "I alone know what is right and what is wrong, and my decision is right." With that he shoos me out the door. I walk back to my hotel mulling over today's unexpected but welcome news, hoping the fighting is over.

During Ghising's absence, headquarters is quiet. Since he refuses to delegate authority, and because his approval is needed for most party activities, everything is stalled. The longer he's away, the more willing people are to confide in me their secret desire for a political solution. "Anyone saying this in public would be cursed, maybe stoned, but I promise you many of us are thinking about compromise," one highly placed GNLF official tells me. He intimates that the most recent fighting has been waged not so much for Gurkhaland, but for a better deal at the negotiating table. He feels that the state and federal governments will never allow Gurkhaland. Formal recognition would set an unwanted precedent, undermining forty years of federal work to convince the country's citizens that they are first and foremost Indians, not Bengalis, Tamils, or Gurkhas. There are scores of separatist movements in multi-ethnic India, and allowing a new state like Gurkhaland would only increase tensions elsewhere. To this official and others who speak to me in whispers, the proposed Hill Council is acceptable.

Like many in Darjeeling, I awake every morning and hasten to the town bulletin board, but no word comes from Ghising. As November wanes, it becomes clear to me that it's time to leave. In more than a month, I've seen only one duck and no rare birds. Maybe these fliers can sense the tension in the hills of Darjeeling and refuse to land near these mountains of trouble. As I'm saying my good-byes, a GVC officer invites me on a three-day excursion.

"Come with us and then leave for New Delhi. We are just going on a training exercise," he says. "Three days . . . There are lakes, rivers. You can walk and look for birds while we train."

I decide to join the eight men crammed into a Land Rover

already full of gear and burlap bags. After a series of bone-rattling jolts, I open the bag I've been using as a pillow. Something hard has been knocking against my head. My hand freezes. The bag is filled with homemade bombs.

"Are you feeling all right?" someone asks. "Sick, eh?" The driver slams on the brakes. Everything flies about, and I find myself cradling the bag, trying to keep the bombs from hitting one another. It takes me several seconds to speak.

"No big deal. Right-o, give them here," the commander says blithely. "We will put them up front." He takes the bag, mistakenly grabbing the bottom and accidentally dumping three bombs. "Bombs away!" he says, laughing. I stand behind the troops, ready to dive for cover as the three deadly balls of jute bounce down the road.

It's pitch black by the time the Rover stops. We make camp several kilometers from the road, and I climb under my blankets soon after dinner. The others sit around the campfire boasting about their sexual prowess. In the early morning, as the GVC practices maneuvers, I wander about with my binoculars. There are plenty of buntings, thrushes, and sparrows, all common birds I could see in Darjeeling, but no ducks. Maybe I'll have better luck when I visit a nearby lake in the afternoon. We regroup to share breakfast, but the meal is interrupted by a messenger from headquarters. The commander looks grim as he reads the dispatch. He calls me over, explaining that they will be staying here the rest of the week. I will return to Darjeeling with the messenger when he finishes his rounds.

"Condition red . . . Positions. NOW!" he orders, turning to his men. As I put my binoculars away and take out my cameras, he yells, "Don't be an idiot with those things. Do you understand me, mister?" He repeats himself inches from my face.

"Yes, sir," I reply, wiping away his spray.

The men stand at attention as the officer checks their weapons and makes a short speech. There will be no more fires, no chatting, and absolutely no bird watching.

On command, the troops pair up and follow the commander to positions overlooking a road. An hour passes without a word being spoken. I wonder how long it will take me to get out of here. The man on my right stares at a picture he has in his wallet. The commander studies a coin, apparently memorizing its every detail. The other men keep their eyes fixed on the road. The forward lookout whistles, and the men hustle for new positions, spreading out. The soldier next to me reloads his gun and plants a kiss on the gunsight. We hear a diesel engine, and seconds later a truck rolls into view carrying a detachment of CRPF troops. The driver downshifts and stops directly below us.

Our commander comes down the line, saying something to each of his men, and even pauses to speak with me. I have to strain to hear his whisper: "This patch of road is a favorite resting place for the CRPF. There is a spring near the edge of the tar."

Lazily the CRPF climb over the tailgate of the truck. I count them as they stretch their legs and joke with each other. There are twenty-two of them and nine of us, including me.

"You stay here and you stay low," the commander orders. "If you see anybody flanking us, shout, damn you, shout."

The Gurkhas creep closer to the unsuspecting CRPF. As ordered, I watch the flanks, shifting around a bit to get a good picture without having my head blown off. I freeze when the commander raises his hands. The men light eight fuses, which sputter as the GVC count down before lobbing the bombs. Two snag in the brush while the other six careen down the slope. *Kaboom! Kaboom!* All eight explode. The startled police leap to their feet and race for cover. The GVC open fire with a salvo of eight whip-cracking sounds. The police return the fire, blindly shooting up the slope at us. Abruptly our commander orders, "Run! Run! Run!"

We sprint madly up the hill, and once we're well beyond range, we pause to catch our breath. I look back through my binoculars, and it appears that all the bombs and bullets have missed their marks. The commander describes the action as "harassment."

"We don't have to kill to scare them."

We set off at a normal pace for a GNLF training camp to the east. The police never trail a Gurkha unit into the hills without heavy reinforcements. The Gurkhas' knowledge of the terrain and their unsurpassed stamina make it foolish. "The hills belong to us," the commander states flatly.

We move in silence, working our way along the boundary of a tea estate. Two hours after the skirmish, we arrive at the training camp, where other patrols are already gathered. I head immediately to the command post to find out when I can leave. The GNLF flag is at half mast. Several gray blankets lie on the ground near the flagpole. I'm a few feet away when a man from another patrol lifts the blankets, one at a time. My stomach knots, tighter and tighter, as each corpse is revealed. A head is nearly trepanned, brains spilling out, flies swarming around the cortex. Next to him is a body with a gaping hole where a leg once was. A hand lies on the chest, but the arm is missing. The third dead man is missing most of his left side. I close his eyes.

"Show the world what the police have done," says one man, who hours before was tossing a bomb.

As I focus my camera, I realize that no picture can capture the horror; any two-dimensional image will only sanitize the experience. There is a smell, putrid and dense; lips caked shut by blood; fingers that will never uncurl; the faces of the survivors contemplating their own fates.

I put down the camera. My breath feels hot and an acrid taste lingers in my throat. As I stare at the bodies, I find myself wishing for a different world.

"Take more pictures," a voice urges.

I walk away. "When can I leave?" I ask the commander. Quickly he rounds up two men to escort me to the road, where I will wait until a jeep loaded with milk stops. The messenger who was supposed to transport me has been detained and this driver has taken his place. As we head to Darjeeling, the man talks excitedly about skirmishes in every part of the district. Both state and Gurkha troops have died, and the area around Kalimpong has seen particularly heavy action. He asserts that the GNLF acted only in retaliation for a brutal police action.

What provoked the police? The driver doesn't know. There has been no progress in New Delhi, he tells me, and I suspect the outburst has been a show of strength by both sides.* Trying to resolve a question haunting me, I ask the driver what Gurkhaland means to him. "Freedom," he replies. "Gurkhaland is freedom, isn't it?"

Late that same night, I'm on the mail train to New Delhi.

---

*The fighting continued for months, but in November 1988, Ghising signed a peace accord, accepting the original offer of a Hill Council.

9

Hindi by Yourself

THE TRAIN RIDE from Darjeeling to New Delhi takes more than forty hours, and as I walk from the station to the Grand Life Hotel, I come upon a puzzling scene: Swedish Christmas carolers, dressed in wool caps and bright red and green costumes, singing in the sweltering sun. One of the singers, a blonde with unusually large hands, doles out samples of eggnog. Bystanders accept them gratefully, but I don't see anyone going back for seconds. Thoughtfully, the Lutheran church has printed a Hindi translation of the Christmas songs. People glance at the lyrics, scratch their heads, and politely return the brochures.

Everyone at the hotel is in a jolly mood, especially Mahout, a sure sign that business has been good.

"Wonderful, things are just wonderful . . . No snags in Bombay, the airport here is cooperating, Calcutta is wide open . . . We are going to celebrate, and you are just in time for the party."

Crates of champagne are stacked in an ice truck hired by Mahout. Workers are decorating the ground floor to resemble a discotheque. The front desk has become a bar, with liquor bottles and glasses covering every square inch. Mirrored globes, strobe lights, bunting, and crystals hang from the ceiling. The caterer, a wiry man in a brown suit much too large for him, fusses over the details.

"Everything must be perfect . . . Mahout has promised me a color TV if he likes it."

The guests start to arrive around seven. Most of the women are wearing elegant cocktail dresses or saris, a few of the daring sport miniskirts; the men are decked out in tuxedos or silk suits, and many flash gold ID bracelets. Mahout, the perfect host, greets each guest warmly.

"Good evening. I'm so glad you could come . . . I would like to introduce you to my new friend, the last great white hunter. Did you know that this man has just . . ."

He then proceeds to exaggerate my adventures, embellishing them with whatever strikes his fancy. "He followed the spoor of the abominable snowman for three weeks . . . He climbed Mount Kanchenjunga without oxygen, says he smoked a pack of cigarettes on the peak . . . subsisted on yak for two months . . ."

Since Mahout refuses to let me pay for my room or anything else, I feel obliged to let him brag all he wants about me. During the course of the evening, various people offer to help me secure a permit for my trip down the Brahmaputra. I decline, assuring them that the paperwork has already reached the highest level. One man persists, however.

"I have much influence," says Jawaharlal by way of introducing himself. He buzzes around me like a horsefly. No doubt he has friends in the government; indeed, many of the guests at the party are politicians or well-placed government officials. Even so, I feel uncomfortable around him. I pull Mahout away from a beautiful woman — no easy task — to ask about Jawaharlal.

"Oh!" he says, looking at the pudgy man and laughing. "He is a good friend. We prepped together. He works for RAW. Right at the top."

"Raw what?"

"R-A-W. Research and Analysis Wing. What you would call a spy."

According to Mahout, RAW is an intelligence organization,

a combined CIA and FBI, monitoring activities inside India as well as around the world.

"What's he doing here?" I ask nervously.

"We all know him and like him . . . You just have to watch what you say."

"But he knows all about my trips! I could get deported!"

"Oh, stop. He is after much bigger fish than you, small fry."

Mahout and Jawaharlal, both strident nationalists, have developed a working relationship. Although they live on different sides of the law, they cross boundaries when they feel national security is at risk.

"We are friends and we are businessmen," Mahout says, "and we are loyal to India."

At ten o'clock the strobe lights come on and the music blares.

"Let's rock," Rani says, taking my hand, leading the way to the center of the dance floor. She looks delicious in a gooseberry-colored sari.

While each night at Mahout's hotel is a new experience, my days are routine. I become expert in lessons 182 through 297 in *Hindi by Yourself,* my latest self-help book. After a morning of bird watching in Lodhi Gardens, a lush oasis right in New Delhi, I usually head to Lok Nayak Bhavan, where I join the office workers on break. I have played enough hands of Indian whist that I'm beginning to win occasionally. My card partners are all from the plains and click their teeth whenever I mention the Himalayas.

"Brrrr. Darjeeling is too cold for me," one man says.

The recent fighting in Darjeeling has made the headlines in Delhi. As far as they're concerned, both the Gurkhas and the state police are wrong.

"What good does a gun do?" asks Prem, the best card player in the group. "If I was in charge, I would make them sit in one room until they worked it out. No one could leave, not even to go to the bathroom . . . Once they find peace, then they could piss."

I've brought the director a present from the hills, a bag of choice Darjeeling tea. He's embarrassed by the gift so, realizing my error, I charge him a dollar. There's no news about my application, and since he knows of no other case like mine, he's unsure what the delay indicates. It may simply be because the minister has been away for a while.

In the late afternoon I often go to the movies. The theaters are open all day and the tickets are cheap. Off Connaught Place there's a cluster of mammoth halls, each fronted by a huge billboard advertising a racy scene in the film. Today I'm lured inside the Odeon by its marquee with a bare-chested man embracing a woman in a tattered dress. His face is painted with iridescent colors, and sparkles have been sprayed across his forehead, glittering beads of celestial sweat. Her ruby lips glisten around a tongue curling like a fresh-cut orange peel.

As in most Indian theaters, there's no box office per se. I simply thrust some money into a small hole in the wall. Out comes a ticket and, when I'm lucky, some change. I walk into the darkened hall and look for an isolated seat. It takes me a couple of minutes to become accustomed to the soundtrack; Indians like it loud.

Today's feature is a typical Hindi movie, produced in Bombay and more than likely written, shot, edited, and released in less than three months. The film is dubbed and the producers probably followed the usual practice of having writers concoct dialogue only hours before the cameras are ready to roll. The plot is simple: boy meets girl, loses her, and miraculously finds her again. The story has several twists, but dramatic flow isn't a priority. In this film, seconds after a tense scene in which the hero is shot by thugs who kidnap his girlfriend, the action shifts to a dream sequence. Hero and heroine are magically transported to an enchanted forest, where other actors, dressed as trees, join them in a song and dance number. Before the credits roll, the hero has killed the bad guys, married his gal, fathered a child, and moved into a marble palace.

However preposterous the plots of most Hindi movies, they may be the most powerful force in New Delhi's effort to make Hindi a truly national language. Pundits claim that film has done more to accomplish this than the entire education system. Perhaps they're right, because in Darjeeling, where Nepalese is the lingua franca, a Gurkha standing outside a theater told me, "They [movies] are the only reason I learned Hindi."

Eight days after my return to Delhi, while browsing in a bookstore, I notice a man flipping through a government study on the rivers of India, a book I've been hunting for. I wait for him to return it to the shelf, but something in the volume catches his eye. He pulls up a stool and settles down.

"Excuse me, are you going to buy that book?" I ask.

"I don't know yet. Why?"

We start talking and introduce ourselves. His name is Shankar Barua, and he suggests that I buy the book and lend it to him. In exchange he graciously offers to buy me a cup of tea.

Shankar describes himself as an artist working as a photographer to make ends meet. "I used to work in Assam," he tells me. "I was a tea broker. I had a car and a membership in a fancy club, but I split that grind to return to my art."

"Assam? Do you know the Brahmaputra?"

"That's why I want the book. I have all these pictures of the river, and I need some words to go with them. The first story did well."

He hands me a magazine. I open it to the dog-eared pages and see his byline on "Down the Brahmaputra," the story of his attempt to paddle the river from near the border of Burma to Bangladesh. On his fourth day out he was attacked by dacoits, and his trip was aborted. He wants to try again, but not alone.

Astounded by this chance encounter, I remember the charms His Holiness gave me in Sikkim. They're in my pocket, and I fondle them as Shankar recounts some childhood memories. He remembers playing on the riverbank near Gauhati, throwing sticks into the channel, imagining their journey to the sea. Often he would dream he was a captain sailing to faraway ports.

"If the dacoits had left me alone, I would have become the first person to travel the river alone from Burma to Bangladesh."

Shankar was born in Assam, the son of a Foreign Service officer. He speaks fluent Assamese and at least three of the myriad dialects of the river people. His father taught him to revere the Brahmaputra, the most powerful of the local gods, telling bedtime stories about the ghosts that hover along the river's edge, waiting in the early morning fog to snatch naughty children.

I gladly accept Shankar's invitation to join his wife and their baby for a meal of spicy Bengali food. Over several hours of conversation, we discover that we share many of the same vices, as well as similar tastes in music and books. I propose that we join forces on a voyage down the river. Each of us has something to offer: Shankar knows the land and the language, and I've got the money and the survival skills.

"Far out, man! This is really something else, eh? Doesn't it blow your mind how we met?" he asks, going on to hum the musical theme of "The Twilight Zone."

Shankar's knowledge of American slang and pop culture is remarkable. As a child growing up in Laos, where his father was posted, he watched armed forces broadcasts from Vietnam. "My parents spoke English, but I learned American by watching Mary Tyler Moore," he says. One of his brothers lives in California, and Poonam, Shankar's wife, works for the American Embassy. Shankar seems to have committed to memory every issue of *People* and *Rolling Stone* magazines. As he says, "What's wrong with trying to keep up?"

He's two years younger than I and eight inches shorter.

Being the son of a diplomat, he has lived all over the world. He came home to Calcutta for college, where, in his words, "I really learned how to party."

For the next week we meet almost every day to make plans and assemble our gear. If I don't get the permit for the Brahmaputra, he assures me that he will go anyway. "You've bought the expensive stuff and I'll think of you when I use it."

On the thirteenth day after leaving Darjeeling, more than three months since my initial visit to Lok Nayak Bhavan, my card-playing friends tell me that the director wants to see me right away. "Good luck," they shout as I fly for the door.

"Quack, quack," goes the guard at the door again, allowing me to barge in front of several dozen people. The director orders tea and tells me to sit.

"This is it. A decision has been made, and I am waiting for your file . . . Do you always smoke two cigarettes at once?" he asks, pointing to the one I've just lit and the one in the ashtray.

Ninety minutes later the messenger arrives with my file, now the size of an auto repair manual. Slowly the director reads the verdict. He stands, offers me his hand, and says, "Congratulations! You got it."

I call Shankar from the bar in a nearby hotel. He can leave in a day. When I spring the news on Mahout, he pulls me to the refrigerator and yanks out a magnum of champagne.

"I've been saving this," he says, beaming.

"To the river!" I toast.

"To Brahma, the Creator," he adds.

10

Lahey-Lahey

HINDUS REVERE the Ganges as the eternal stream of life, mother of all rivers, heavenly water to nourish the body and purge the soul; the Brahmaputra, son of Brahma, is her consort. Born in the Himalayas almost within sight of one another, the two rivers flow in opposite directions, gather strength, and loop back to merge into one. Their paths form a giant circle marking the center of the physical universe for Buddhists and Hindus alike.

The Brahmaputra has many incarnations along its 2,900-kilometer path through Tibet, India, and Bangladesh, its name changing from place to place, culture to culture. In Tibet, where it rises and is known as the Zangbo, or "the Purifier," it flows eastward, coursing 1,800 kilometers parallel to the main ridge of the Himalayas. It's navigable for a third of that length, and riverboats zigzag along it two miles above sea level, as close to the stars as a sailor can be.

The river swings south near Mêdog, entering India in grand fashion, tumbling down gorges and rock canyons hewn by the lesser gods as a present to Brahma. Picking up speed as it loses altitude, the river, now called the Dihang, races through the Mishmi Hills. At the tip of the Assam Valley, near Saikhoa Ghat, it assumes its familiar, ancient name and heads west, reversing course to chase the setting sun. Here it widens to ten miles in spots, slowing and spreading out as the land flattens. After entering Bangladesh, the river is known by three different names, the most famous being Padma, an avatar birthed near the river's confluence with the Ganges.

Shankar and I have decided to begin our voyage in Saikhoa Ghat, a small village in the northeast corner of Assam, near Burma. Getting there from New Delhi gives new meaning to the phrase "down time." I'm tipped off early by the man sitting next to me on the plane ride to Gauhati, the capital of Assam, that this is going to be a long flight. Minutes after we board, he opens a book. Noticing my inquisitive glance, he holds up the jacket of the thick volume: *Great Russian Novels*, a Reader's Digest compilation of condensed classics.

"Enjoying it?" I ask.

"Very much. I read the first half, *War and Peace*, on the flight to Delhi. Would you like it when I finish?"

When the plane arrives, seven hours late, I disembark carrying the abridged Russian epics.

It's two in the morning when we pull up outside the Barua family home. The lights are out. Everyone must have gone to bed, sure that we had missed the plane. Shankar heads for the light switch. I hit a chair, toppling it, and crash to the floor.

"Who's there?" an alarmed voice demands.

Every light in the house pops on. Shankar's brother Kumar is the first to appear. In short order he's followed by Shankar's mother, sister-in-law, and older brother.

"I knew it," says Kumar. "I knew it had to be you. No burglar could make that much noise."

Kumar, twenty-seven, is the youngest of the four Barua boys. A little taller than Shankar and twenty pounds heavier, he's wearing a nightshirt that brushes the ground, protecting his legs from the mosquitoes. When we sit down to eat, he joins us, while the others return to bed.

The house is large by Indian standards, having four bedrooms and a spacious living room. Its decor reflects their life in the diplomatic corps. One wall is covered with mementos of Russia, another displays curios from Indochina, South America, and Europe. A collection of Venetian glass is showcased only inches from the chair I toppled during my entrance. On the mantelpiece is a picture of Shankar's parents at a shipyard near the Black Sea. His mother is just about to christen the first ship built by the Soviets for the Indian Navy.

Like Shankar, his brothers speak perfect idiomatic English, spiking their language with American slang and cockney expressions. Next morning, when we eat breakfast together, I talk to Amar, the oldest son, who owns a chicken farm. He's never heard of the pink-headed duck, but he offers some practical advice: "Use cornmeal to capture one. I will breed it with a pochard. We'll make millions."

The bus to upper Assam doesn't leave until sunset, but I drag Shankar to the Blue Hills Bus Terminal early in the afternoon. The depot is packed. A large TV sits on a platform high above the vinyl floor, dominating the room. The sound is off, but a soap opera flickers on the screen. I'm rather pleased that I can distinguish five different languages being spoken around us. Shankar isn't impressed; he can pick out twice that number, and he reminds me that a hundred and fifty languages and more than five hundred dialects are spoken in India.

Bunched in one corner is a group of Naga tribespeople, who appear to love primary colors, the purer the better. They wear red hats, blue shawls, yellow pants or skirts. Their speech is guttural, composed of many consonants and harsh sounds. Naga profiles reflect the look of their ancestral Shan cousins from Thailand and Burma. To me, the women are stunning, especially their alluring eyes, large black pearls floating in delicate cream faces.

In the middle of the room there's a party of tribespeople from Arunachal Pradesh, the wildest and least populated state of India. One of the men is whittling, putting the finishing touches on a small stylized panther, I think, or maybe a tiger. He doesn't seem to mind when I squat next to him. Using sign language, I try to ask him about his carving. Bewildered, he shakes his head and keeps on working. Shankar tries a Mishmi dialect. Finally a bystander offers to translate.

"Is it a cat?" I ask.

"No, bear."

"Will he sell it?"

"Yes."

"How much?"

"He wants your pants."

"They are the only ones I have. Will he take a knife? A flashlight?"

"No. He wants your pants. He says you can keep that cheap stuff. Pants or nothing."

"How about money?"

"No. Money is useless in the hills. Now he says he wants your pants and a carton of cigarettes."

He keeps the sculpture but convinces me to give him a pack of cigarettes. Shankar and I wander outside. The smell of something burning draws us toward an alley. Upwind from a flaming trash can is a group of Meghalayans, all wearing rubber shoes and carrying waterproof bags. They offer us tea. The leader tells Shankar that they're going home to Cherrapunji, which is just eighty miles south of here and is the wettest spot on earth. It holds two world records for rainfall: in one day 41 inches fell, and in one year more than 850 inches fell.

As we drink tea, the headman keeps nudging me and pointing at an embarrassed teenaged girl, his daughter. Reluctantly she heeds his command to sit next to me. I'm intrigued by her silver earrings, which nibble her lobes like schools of minnows. Her father orders her to remove one, and as she does, her personality changes dramatically. No longer shy, she starts bartering in a quick, loud voice, sure of herself. Her father beams as we conclude the deal: one earring for a wrist-radio, a knife, two bandannas, five Godzilla pins, a box of plastic toothpicks, and ten rupees. Later Shankar tells me that the earring is worth only three or four rupees.

The dispatcher announces our bus, and we hurry to load our luggage. Shankar curses when he sees the large letters on the coach proclaiming "Super Video Luxury."

"What does that mean?"

"Pain," he replies and covers his ears.

Each of these buses is equipped with one videotape, which is played over and over for the length of the trip, about fifteen hours in our case. I retrieve my medical kit and pull out a handful of cotton for my ears. After other passengers ask for some, I approach the driver.

"Nobody wants to see the movie a dozen times. Why not show it once or twice?"

"Impossible. The machine is supposed to be on the whole time. This is a Super Video Coach!"

We leave the city limits as the sun dips behind the horizon. The lower half of the sky is a sickly yellow, but the upper portion, above the dense smog, is a vibrant orange. We follow Route 37, a two-lane road running along the left bank of the Brahmaputra. After the second replay of the movie, I doze off, stirring only when the bus pulls up to an all-night restaurant with a parking lot filled with trucks and other buses. Everyone here seems to be in a hurry. Passengers wolf down their food, and the restaurant staff quickly lose patience with those who can't make up their minds. Twice I'm ordered out of line and finally decide to eat whatever Shankar orders.

"Duta Diya," I say — make that two — my first Assamese phrase.

We continue on, zooming eastward along flat terrain. Finally the morning light bleaches the video screen, dissolving the image into benign obscurity. On both sides of the bus are tea estates, giants in comparison to those in Darjeeling. Shankar tells me that Assam produces the bulk of Indian tea. While

Darjeeling grows a high-quality leaf that imparts subtle flavor, the Assamese crop is known for its strong, pungent taste. Plentiful and cheap, it's the tea of the people.

We debark in Tinsukia, a town that served as a staging area for American troops during World War II. Metal signs advertising American products of the 1940s are still in place. One billboard, its paint peeling, depicts a man who bears a striking resemblance to a young Ronald Reagan, exhaling a cloud of smoke. "I like the pack. I love the taste," says the slogan, going on to urge "victory."

Shankar and I switch buses for Saikhoa Ghat. The new bus, owned and operated by the state, has no battery and must be jump-started. We and the other passengers push it for almost a kilometer of fits and false starts; with a belch of black smoke, the engine finally comes to life. We climb aboard and drive past acre after acre of tea bushes until, suddenly, anything green vanishes. Pfft! The vegetation stops, replaced by a brown and lifeless plain.

"The flood line," the driver explains.

He whistles as the hot air blows in our faces and deposits a thin layer of sand over everything. It's high noon. The only breaks in the monotonous landscape are the stark remains of animals drowned by the monsoon flood. Two months ago this land was submerged under several feet of river.

A half hour later we stop near a clump of rickety bamboo structures. Saikhoa Ghat? The driver nods. This is it or, more accurately, what's left of it after this year's monsoon. A new settlement and ferry landing have been established about three kilometers downstream, and the latest reincarnation of Saikhoa Ghat is growing up around it. A middle-aged man with a boil under his left ear grabs our bags the moment we put them down. "Which way?" he asks. Rather than arguing, we hire him to lead us to the ghat. Thirty minutes later I stare wide-eyed into the Brahmaputra.

The river is an ocean. To the north there's not a speck of

land. The wind is blowing at fifteen knots, and whitecaps dot the blue expanse. Overhead the clouds have stretched to near nothingness. Shankar continues walking, but I linger, holding my hands over the surface to feel the reflected heat of the sun. As I dip my fingers into the water, I whisper to the river god. In the distance a gull screeches and banks in the pale sky.

I catch up with Shankar in the middle of town, a dusty place with sixteen flimsy buildings in a row. There are no streets, only footpaths in the sand. Chickens wander about, and several mangy dogs lie in the sun, panting. A fleet of small boats is hauled up on the mud shore, and several fishing nets, hoisted on long poles, snap in the breeze. Groups of men drink tea in the shade of the bamboo, thatch, and rope structures. Not one nail has been used. When the next monsoon threatens, the owners will be ready to take apart their shops and truck the pieces to higher ground.

On his previous trip Shankar made friends with Moti, the owner of a teahouse. He greets Shankar with a hug, then turns to me. He straightens, clicks his unshod heels in military fashion, and extends his hand.

"Now we are friends," he says after we shake.

As he serves us tea, flies buzz around his butter-greased hair.

"Anything you want, Moti can get," he whispers.

"Don't tempt us," Shankar replies.

"I am your friend and want to please you," he says, quoting prices three or four times the usual black-market rate.

Like most people who work the river, Moti spends eight or nine months here in Assam and then returns home to his wife and children in Bihar during the monsoon season. The local Assamese tribes live in the hills year-round, having abandoned the floodplain centuries ago. Moti knows little about the hills or mountains; he knows the water. He shipped out as an apprentice cook before he was seven.

"It was a surprise to me," he recalls. "I was one of six

children, and I knew something was about to happen when my mother brought me a sweet and no one else got one. That night my father told me about my new job. I left the next morning."

By the time he was sixteen he had saved enough money to start his first teahouse. He has lost everything six times, four times to the river and twice to a better hand of cards.

"Shiva has many tests for me. This year I returned and could not find my shop. Not a stick was left. I had to borrow to build this," he says, pausing to look heavenward before asking, "Does the American play cards?"

Three long blasts of a steam whistle announce the arrival of the ferry. Several times a day, depending on the weather and currents, a sixty-two-foot boat chugs steadily across the river to Sadiya, gateway to the rugged and largely unexplored Mishmi Hills. There are fewer than twenty passengers aboard, but the water laps the starboard rail under the weight of a cargo of teak logs. As the captain supervises the unloading, he sees me lurking near the bow and waves me aboard.

At first he confuses me with someone else. "A white *firang* [foreigner] boarded my ferry seven or eight years ago," he says before inviting me on a tour. He purchased the boat years ago at auction in Calcutta. It used to be a workboat servicing the fleet of British steamships that plied the Brahmaputra during the first half of the century. He's intimate with every detail of her lines and scantlings. To his eye there's no prettier vessel on the river. As he shows me the engine, he uses his shirttail to wipe a gob of oil from the valve cover. The hull, launched in Glasgow, is double-planked, and her heavy oak ribs indicate that she was most likely built for the North Sea. This boat will undoubtedly outlive its captain, a fact not lost on him.

"She has the beauty of a river goddess and the spirit of Ram. I want my ashes scattered from her stern."

When I describe our plans to buy a small boat and paddle

the length of the river, the captain puts his arm around me like a father and leads me to the bridge. Pointing downstream, he warns me about the dacoits who control a 150-kilometer stretch of the river called the Badlands.

"Between Jorhat and Tezpur is the worst. The Nareesch gang is there . . . Why does a firang want to do this?"

I explain my search for the pink-headed duck, and suddenly my intentions make sense to him. He can understand a pilgrimage, no matter what it's for. As a boy, he tells me, he journeyed with his father to Mount Kailas, the hallowed fortress of Shiva in the northern Himalayas. The trip remains his most vivid childhood memory.

"Yes, you must do these things. The gods will protect you."

I take out a map and ask about the uncharted area near Burma. He scratches his head while studying the map, speckling it with dandruff.

"That is no place to find a duck. Look on the river, not in the hills."

Later I take out my Polaroid and gather the willing ferry crew for a portrait. The photo is a hit, and I ask them if they know of any boats for sale, offering individual portraits if they locate one. In less than an hour a crewman introduces me to Jodu Das. Short and well built, he's wearing a lungi and a plaid shirt knotted at the waist. Jodu leads me to his boat.

The moment I see his skiff, I know it's the one for us. Of the two dozen crafts moored near the landing, it alone appears speedy and maneuverable; certainly it's the smallest and has the narrowest beam, good for paddling but inadequate for fishing. I check for dry rot with my knife and find none, so for forty-six dollars I become the owner of a twelve-foot skiff equipped with paddles and push poles. Shankar writes out the sales agreement in Assamese, Hindi, and English. I ink Jodu's thumb with the tip of a magic marker and sign below his mark.

With everyone at the ghat watching, Shankar and I climb aboard and shove off for a test run. Within seconds we spin out of control and nearly capsize. It takes us a while to regain our balance and any semblance of control. We finally manage to steer a straight course, but when we turn to head upstream, we're unable to make headway against the current. We land about a mile downstream and tow the boat back to the ghat. The gallery hushes as we near; no doubt our display has them laying down bets, setting odds on how long we will survive.

Jodu Das never gave the boat a name, but Shankar insists on one. Splashing water over the bow, he christens her *Lahey-Lahey,* meaning "Slowly slowly" in Assamese.

Moti prepares a feast, which in this area means anything other than fish and rice. A dozen of us share a thin chicken stew. I sit next to the captain, who jokes that our inexperience will do us in before the dacoits have a chance. I tell him that I've sailed alone across oceans, but he's not impressed.

"The Brahmaputra is more than an ocean. It is a god you must fear. The river swallows boats."

After dinner I walk with the captain back to his ferry. We stand in the moonlight on the aft deck, looking up at the stars. Saturn is about to set, and Jupiter dominates Andromeda; the Great Bear in Ursa Major crowds the northern edge of the heavens; Polaris hangs twenty-eight degrees above the horizon, marking our latitude.

"They say each star is a saint," the captain muses. "Someday I hope to be a star . . . Why not come with us tomorrow? See the river from the other side."

I accept the offer.

In the morning a heavy dew slicks every outdoor surface. Great veils of mist rise from the river. It's absolutely clear a few feet inland, but visibility over the water is less than a boat's length. Moti tells me that the river gods are hiding themselves while they bathe. In a stern voice he warns me never to paddle before the gods perform their morning ablutions.

"It is dangerous to see the gods naked," he says, wagging a finger.

I'm one of the first people to queue up for the ferry and almost the only one not restraining an animal. When the loading ramp is in place, the civility of the line disappears. Passengers rush forward, pushing and shoving, dragging their livestock, trying to secure their favorite spots on deck. The whistle sounds, and the crewmen scurry to their stations. When the engine is turned on, it sends tremors through the decking. The rumbling brings smiles to the faces of the passengers and grunts of terror from the animals. The captain climbs down from the bridge and heads to the bow, stopping now and then when he recognizes a commuter. At the prow he stands to port, faces the mighty river, and whispers a prayer. He produces an orange from under his shawl and lobs it into the water. It's important, he says later, to start each day with an offering to Brahma.

"What happens if you don't?" I ask.

"You will never have to remember anything again . . . This is His river."

Back in the wheelhouse the captain orders the mate to cast off. The mooring lines are released and the boarding plank shipped. The engine slips into gear and the ferry lurches forward. It's a perfect day for a boat ride, with little wind and lots of blue sky. River terns circle us, diving for anything thrown over the side.

Off the starboard quarter, bobbing in the water a kilometer away, I notice a flock of brahminy ducks, sacred to Buddhists as symbols of fidelity and devotion. These ducks mate for life; when one dies, the other stays near the corpse until it, too, dies. I have an urge to commandeer the boat for a closer look at the ducks, and Brahma smiles on me — the captain taps me on the shoulder and asks if I would like to take the wheel.

"Hey! Where are you going? . . . Steer for that island up ahead," he commands, spinning the wheel in my hands and taking us away from the birds.

There's a strong weather helm, and I need to feather the rudder constantly to keep us from sideslipping. As we pass into the main channel, the bow swings, caught in the rip. I put the wheel hard over, but the current, surging downstream at five or six knots, is too strong. The skipper pulls a string that runs down through a hole in the deck to a bell in the engine room, alerting the engineer to open the throttle. Slowly we regain control.

Hooked above a chart table littered with bread crumbs and dirty tea cups is a length of cardboard tubing, the ferry's external communication system. The captain has no use for a radio; the tube is all he has ever needed. "It always works," he says. "And if I had a radio, who would I talk to?"

There's a compass aboard, but he's never had it adjusted. I compare my field compass to it and find an eighteen-degree discrepancy on a northeast heading. It doesn't matter, his compass is more an ornament than a navigation instrument. The captain steers by eye and instinct, relying on his thirty-odd years of experience and a sailor's sixth sense. "I can feel danger coming . . . Something happens inside me."

In the middle of the river, almost three miles out from Saikhoa Ghat, hard by a cluster of small islands, the captain retakes the helm. He tugs the line twice, and the engine slows. "Shallows," he warns, staring ahead, surveying every ripple. A bowman takes soundings as we move cautiously through a narrow strait between the barren islands. Using a long pole, the bowman calls out the general conditions: deep, shallow, or shoal. Because it carries almost as much water as two Mississippis, the Brahmaputra is a navigator's nightmare. Overnight the river may dump hundreds of acres' of silt into an area, choking it off and diverting the main stream. Every morning the captain must survey the river anew, paying close attention to the wave patterns, which give clues to the bottom contour; generally, the steeper the wave, the shallower the water. The captain tells me that the Brahmaputra is a moody god whose every whim must be indulged. To make his point, he jerks the rope four times and stamps hard on the deck twice, the signal to clutch the engine. He leads me to the windward rail. "Listen," he tells me. "Listen to the water and feel its power."

I stand there motionless, captivated by the sound of the river gnawing at the islands. It's a deep, ominous drone, interrupted by occasional splashes as pieces of the bank, undermined by erosion, tumble into the river.

"Look, off to starboard!" the captain shouts, and sprints for the wheel. He calls for full power.

From upstream several trees the size of telephone poles are bearing down on us like battering rams. They could easily punch a hole through the ferry, and I shudder at the thought of what they could do to *Lahey-Lahey*. We successfully avoid them and continue on for Sadiya, the ancient port where Tibetans once came to trade gold dust, musk, and borax for cloth, tobacco, and glass.

We make a perfect landing, the bow gently nudging the bank, and three crewmen jump ashore to handle the mooring lines. The ferry will return in two or three hours, depending on how quickly the cargo of teak is loaded.

"Stay close," the captain advises. "We leave when we leave."

I wander about the ghat, which is bustling in comparison to its sister across the river. Several motorized craft are docked along the bank, including another ferry and a trio of barges used to transport logs to the plywood and veneer factories downriver. Like Saikhoa Ghat, Sadiya is populated largely by people from outside Assam, mostly from Bihar and West Bengal. As I sit in a teahouse talking to a group of wharfingers, a tall gentleman wearing khaki pants and a clean white shirt confronts me.

"Who are you?" he butts in.

A man sitting next to me whispers, "Police." I quickly fish out my papers, and the tall man makes the most of this rare chance to display his authority. He orders me to follow him to his office, but once we're inside, he graciously offers me a seat and starts boiling water for tea. Finding my papers in order, he asks me to enter my name in his visitors' log. I drink two cups of tea while he searches for it.

"Would you help me look?" he asks, pointing to a tea crate filled with mildewed paper.

"When did you last use it?"

"Ummm. Let me think. It was before I was married . . . I have two children now."

Giving up, he hands me a blank piece of paper to sign. He fills in all the information from my travel permits and tells me I can leave.

Back at the ferry ghat, I climb atop a huge stack of logs to survey the waterfront. Shirtless laborers are hefting sixty-kilo bags of rice off the ferry to waiting bullock carts; rice dust leaking from the sacks has turned the men a ghostly white. Occasionally a worker will step out of line and stare longingly at the herd of water buffalo cooling in the river. Off to my right, near a parked convoy of logging trucks, a platoon of soldiers banters good-naturedly, glad to be heading home on leave. Downstream, fishermen dip hand nets relentlessly, always seeming to come up empty. Directly below me, two dogs bark as if they've treed dinner. Using my binoculars, I look for birds. There are no marshes nearby; I see only terns, kingfishers, little egrets, and gulls.

"Can I look?" a voice asks. It's the policeman again.

As I climb down, he chases away the dogs, throwing rocks with startling accuracy and speed. He says he's the bowler on the local cricket team. The moment he raises the glasses, all work stops and a line forms. Everyone wants a peek. Happily, the policeman assumes control, allotting each person exactly fifteen seconds with the binoculars. This gives me an opportunity to inquire about the duck; I wave the picture and start asking questions, which are met with vacant stares and frozen smiles. I speak louder and make some changes in my enunciation. Everyone laughs.

"You were right the first time," the policeman says, correcting my use of a slang word for penis. "What was it you were asking about? A rose . . . what?"

"The pink-headed duck, gūlāb-sīr."

"A Mishmi might know about the bird," he says, and sends a young boy on an errand.

Moments later the boy returns with an old gentleman in tow. His name means "Warrior with the Strength of a Thousand." I'm told that in his youth, this Mishmi was a great hunter, reputed to have killed a bear with his hands. He looks blankly at the picture.

"Same color," he says, pointing to his beautiful necklace of polished cowrie shells. "I want one. Does the firang sell these birds?"

"I'm looking for one. Have you ever seen any?"

"Ducks live there," he says, gesturing downstream, turning on his heel, and heading back to his cook fire. "I am hungry now," he adds over his shoulder.

The sound of a horn brings my attention back to the ghat. It's the ferry signaling all aboard. On the way back to Saikhoa Ghat, the captain plots a different course. He lets me steer much of the way, taking the helm only near the shallows. We weave through a series of flat islands, hugging one bank and then the other, always searching for deep water. Even with the engine in gear, throttle two-thirds ahead, I can hear the river devouring chunks of the islands. I head aft for a better listening post. On the fantail a dozen goats hang their heads over the rail as two herders milk them. I'm offered a cup of warm milk, and the children laugh at my chalky mustache. As we approach the ghat, I spot Shankar bailing out *Lahey-Lahey*. Jodu Das is standing nearby wringing his hands.

"I must tell you something," Jodu says sheepishly.

"We have a leak," Shankar interjects.

"We must fix it," Jodu admits.

Several cracks in the stern have been stuffed with oakum and tarred to look like the rest of the bottom. After inspecting it, I decide it's not a serious problem, and if it becomes one, we can fix it easily enough. Jodu insists, however, and the three of us tow *Lahey-Lahey* to an area called the shipyard, a flat stretch of beach littered with boats awaiting repairs. We find the shipwright working on Jodu's new craft. His name is Hayna. When he's introduced he snorts and returns to work. His tool box contains a hammer, saw, drawknife, plane, adze, breast drill, and a length of iron bar known as "the persuader."

"That is all I need to build a boat," Hayna tells me proudly.

Jodu must speak to him in private before he will agree to sell us a bucket of pitch. Shankar heats the tar over a fire while I cut copper strips to cover the bigger gaps in the planks. The shipwright watches me with a critical eye. He stops grimacing only after he has elbowed me out of the way. To correct my shoddy job, he moves the patches a millimeter and nails them home. Together we swab the hull with pitch, trying to get as even a surface as possible. While the sun bakes the goo, Shankar and Jodu return to the ghat, while I stay to watch Hayna frame his latest creation.

Like most other master builders, Hayna appreciates an audience as long as they stay quiet and out of the way. He builds boats the same way his father and grandfather did. The designs are ancient, and the scantlings are a family secret. He takes his time, studying each piece of wood, feeling the texture and tracing the grain. To him a boat is a living organism with personality and character, both of which he shapes.

"What do you think about boats made of steel?" I ask.

"No good. They sink," he replies between chops of his adze. "A boat must be made of wood."

"Why?"

"Can't drive a nail through steel."

That night Shankar and I host our own bon voyage party. The entire ghat turns up at Moti's when they hear I'm paying for the food and supplying the liquor. We down several bottles of scotch, more than enough to have the good spirits of Lord Johnnie Walker bless us all. After tea the next morning, we start loading *Lahey-Lahey*. Hayna is there to offer advice.

"Never travel in the rain . . . Giant fish and crocodiles attack during storms . . . Pray to Ram when you see a whirlpool. He may hear you and save you . . . Keep your fire bright. Ghosts fear light. Do you have flashlights? . . . When the moon is up, sleep with your knives . . ."

He stops, nodding in approval, when I hold out two pieces of fruit. Shankar takes one and we make an offering to Brahma, invoking his spirit to guide us safely to the sea. The oranges splash and bob downstream, carrying our prayer ahead of us. The people of Saikhoa Ghat wave and shout as we climb aboard. The captain blasts the ferry's whistle as we dip our paddles. We clear the back-eddy along the bank and enter the main channel of the god.

I I

Down the Brahmaputra

Lahey-Lahey is ten feet at the water line and a little under twelve feet overall. At her beamiest she's an elbow-bruising thirty inches. There's little pitch to her and no sheer to speak of; the rails run straight from the bow to the blunt stern. On an even keel our weight drops the gunwale to within inches of the water. There are no thwarts, so Shankar kneels on our tent in the bow, while I steer from the V-shaped transom, my feet in the bilge with our bailing can, an old fruit cocktail tin. The push poles lie fore and aft, hanging over the stern like a swallow's tail.

Our first day out, we're lucky to have kind seas and a following wind. We decide to hug the left bank and learn through trial and error how to handle *Lahey-Lahey*. Hour by hour our incompetence lessens: we're getting the hang of it.

As Shankar tells me, "It's rhythm, man. It's all about rhythm. We've just got to hold the beat."

Early in the afternoon we finally hit our stride, pulling as if linked by a cog, matching strokes, propelling *Lahey-Lahey* in a smooth, steady motion. I lose myself in this new world gliding past. The splash of the oars cutting the surface captures my attention, drawing me in like a mantra. I feel the energy flowing from the blade into my arms and through my body, bonding me to the river, freeing me from thought.

After a while, Shankar slips his paddle and leans back. Gazing skyward, he lights a cigarette and releases a stream of smoke.

"Wow! This is really far out, isn't it?" he remarks, instantly dispelling the magic.

I keep pulling, reminded of why I usually travel alone. He says something else, but the splash of my paddle drowns him out. "Hey," he shouts, turning to confront me. I keep at it, plunging the oar deep into the water, pulling back with all my might.

"Hey, listen to me when I'm talking," Shankar yells. A moment later, we're screaming at each other. It's our first tiff, which is quickly resolved, both of us satisfied that *Lahey-Lahey* has no captain, just two crewmen ready to mutiny at any sign of authority.

Hundreds of islands dot my chart of the Brahmaputra, but the chart is inaccurate: there are thousands of islands, ranging from giants large enough to support a forest to small, desolate mounds. A river island's lifespan may be less than a week or more than a century. Only one thing is certain: the river is the sole creator. The process of island making, known as braiding, starts as the Brahmaputra slows and widens across the alluvial plain. After being suspended in the turbid water sluicing down mountain courses, millions of cubic meters of soil and eroded rock begin to settle. Sand bars grow into islands, and as the riverbed recontours around these new land masses, the main channel shifts. During the monsoon season this process accelerates and islands are born in hours, only to disappear in the next thunderclap.

As we shoot down a gut separating the left bank from the nearest islands, the horizon on all sides is a flat vista, not even a dune interrupting the horizontal plane. But rather than an expansive feeling, a sense of emptiness creeps into me, as if I'm slowly draining into the stark landscape. The river surface mirrors the high sun, white-hot and throbbing. The oppressive heat pounds down on my neck, and the hot, sticky breeze is like a dog's breath.

Several miles downstream, just as we clear a long spit, I see a dull green in the distance, which brightens from olive to boa as we get closer. It's the jungle, and we paddle hard for it, pulling double time. We race by a reed-covered island and continue stroking until we reach the coolness of the jungle shadow. There's a twenty-degree temperature drop in the deep, luxurious shade cast by the wild tangle of the rain forest. Cruising contentedly alongside the lush vegetation, we revel in the varying light caused by gaps in the gumhar, kuthan, and gular trees. The arching root systems of the giant teaks, the cathedrals of the jungle, are streaked with red and blue fungi. Yellow-flowered creepers twist around the willows, and the stringy branches of a Persian lilac droop over the bank. Some smaller trees have fallen, and their exposed root balls are now tenanted by sandpipers and redshanks. We can hear insects clicking and monkeys whooping. No doubt word is out about the two men in a boat.

We spot a few tracks in the mud and stop to inspect them. This stretch of river, unpopulated by humans, is home to slow lorises, panthers, leopards, fishing cats, and tigers. The prints are too small for a tiger, but they could be those of a golden cat or a clouded leopard. Shankar carries the slingshot and leads the way.

"What do you think made these?" I ask.

"Big cats, big daddycats . . . I don't know. You're supposed to be Mister Natural, remember? But check this out," he says heading toward some exotic-looking brown orchids. Each bloom has a wide lip bearded with fine, dark hairs. Flowers, it turns out, are Shankar's weak spot. He leans over my shoulder as I flip through a field guide trying to identify the two-leaved orchid.

"It's a *Coelogyne ovalis*," I say. "Rare outside of this area." He starts to pick one, but I stop him, suggesting he pluck the more common *Dendrobium* orchids. He fills his buttonholes with these flowers, dismissing the Latin name of the plant and insisting that we call it "heartbeat" because of its crimson spots, which pulse in the slightest breeze.

"Hey, watch your step," I shout.

In his rush to snip the delicate stems, he doesn't notice he's trampling a lady-slipper, a *Paphiopedilum fairieanum*. We inspect the ballerina grace of this pink flower, first discovered in Assam in 1857. A few specimens were shipped to England, but by 1880, because of poor techniques of propagation, there wasn't one left in Europe. Attempts to relocate the orchid in India failed and a hefty reward was offered. Thirty-five years passed before an expedition of botanists rediscovered the lady-slipper growing in Bhutan.

"Wouldn't you know it. We're a day late and a dollar short," Shankar says ruefully.

I return to the tracks that brought us here in the first place.

"Let's go before whatever it is returns," Shankar says, tossing me the slingshot and climbing aboard *Lahey-Lahey.*

A few miles farther on, birds crowd the view: kingfishers hover near the water; gray-headed fishing eagles soar effortlessly overhead; mynas, swallows, and plovers, with high-pitched voices and bright colors, dart in and out of the jungle. Cormorants dive for dinner while a flock of pochards bob like corks. From their roost on a tree limb high above the bank, a pair of yellow-backed sunbirds welcome us with their call, "Cheech-a-wee, cheech-a-wee." At last I've found an area in which the pink-headed duck could prosper.

We stop for a late lunch, picking a river island with a good view of the jungle. It's a treeless mound of sand rising from the water like a humpbacked whale. Hundreds of empty, waterlogged nests are scattered about. This year, a month after the monsoon was thought to have ended, it rained for two weeks straight. The sun would reappear briefly, only to be blotted out again by more rain. The river flooded a second time, inundating this island and more than likely forcing the birds to abandon their nests.

The island's written history begins with an entry in my log. What I observe gains credibility with each additional sentence and soon acquires a remarkable similarity to fact. I manage to pace off nearly half of its width before getting bored with precision and resorting to estimate, concluding that the island is exactly three square acres, with an elevation of thirty-three inches, precisely matching the inseam of my pants. I dub this grassless place Kojak Island and stake my claim.

All at once it comes to me that I've paddled off the map, into the unknown. The river is constantly changing, shifting direction and speed, meandering along a path chosen by the gods. Walking to the edge of the water, I give the call of the pink-headed duck.

"Quack-quirk-quack-quirk-quirk."

"That's the pink duck's call?" Shankar asks, puzzled.

"Pretty close," I assure him.

"You sure?"

"Positive."

We dine on my favorite staples: tea, chocolate, and cookies. Energized by the caffeine and sugar, I plunge naked into the icy water of the Brahmaputra. Shankar joins me in the water for a few minutes and emerges with chattering teeth. We both resolve to postpone our next bath until we're much farther downstream.

For the next leg of the journey, we switch places in the boat, eager to verify our suspicions that the other has had the easier job and the more comfortable seat. We're both wrong. There's no such thing as comfort aboard *Lahey-Lahey*. Shankar has a difficult time steering and I'm inept as a bowman. Within two miles we return to our original positions.

In the distance stand the giant radio towers of Dibrugarh, the first signs of humanity we've seen since leaving Saikhoa Ghat. To avoid meeting other boats, we elect to head across the river for the unsettled north bank. As we paddle through a string of midstream islands, we happen upon a kingdom of ducks. Swimming in the calm water, protected from the wind and safe from shore predators, are thousands upon thousands of waterfowl. Flocks of spotbills and little grebes arch their necks as we coast by. At the edge of a flock a lookout squawks the alarm. At once there's the frantic tumult of wings and the soft patter of webbed feet racing across the water's surface. The ducks lift off, row after row, perfectly choreographed, their fluttering mass obscuring the sun. Like a pesky insect, we move through the flocks, watching the dance again and again.

I see splashes of emerald, red, and blue feathers, plenty of downy white, and lots of speckles, but not one flash of sunset pink. Once, an odd duck in a flock of pochards catches my eye. Back-paddling, I spin *Lahey-Lahey* around and use the push pole to head for the duck, only to discover that it's a widgeon preening its dull, brownish-pink feathers.

We leave the midstream islands as the sun is about to set. The north bank is a plain of sand rolling all the way to the distant Miri Hills. We're content to spend the night in this lonely spot, away from man and far from the jungle with its leeches and inquisitive cats. Establishing the campsite, however, is a classic study in bumbling, a lost episode of "Gilligan's Island." Our tent is simply a rectangle of plastic, which in theory can be erected in a couple of minutes; all we have to do is arch several lengths of split bamboo and stretch the plastic over them. That first night it takes us nearly an hour to master the technique. We have better luck with the stove, an old three-gallon mustard oil container with one side cut out and the top crimped to hold a cook pot.

That night the stars belong to us alone. Shankar claims the western sky, a bejeweled space dominated by Orion and Capella, with Auriga and Gemini close by. Castor and Pollux, the twin patrons of sailors and travelers, shine bright. My starry domain to the east holds the elegant necklaces of Draco,

Lyra, and Pegasus. Hercules stands at the border of the north-west horizon, with the Phoenix perched at the southern extreme.

At bedtime I discover a critical flaw in the design of the tent: it's too short. My feet extend eight inches out into the damp air. I mention this to Shankar, architect of our home, who is already snug inside a sleeping bag fit for an assault on Everest. He says the tent is perfect, exactly the length of his own body. Like our boat, the tent has little room inside, forcing us to lie shoulder to shoulder.

A little after dawn, with visibility less than three yards, we paddle into a vaporous world cluttered with sounds, many unidentifiable. Every spoken word has a slight echo. The paddles are supernaturally loud, slapping rather than slipping into the water. *Lahey-Lahey*'s planks creak and groan, but it's the other noises coming from somewhere in the fog that make us anxious. There's a splash to starboard, and a second later another to port. Something gurgles and seems to circle us. We hear birds all around, but we can't see them until they're a few inches away, just as startled as we are. It's my job to steer, but moments after shoving off, I lose sight of the bank and must assure Shankar that my impeccable sense of direction will keep us on course.

"Don't you want to use a compass?" Shankar asks a little farther on, noting that the waves are crossing our bow.

"The wind must have shifted. We're heading the right way. Onward."

Blindly we continue. At last, three hours after we cast off, the sun burns away the fog, and we find ourselves back on the south bank of the river, heading directly for the radio towers of Dibrugarh.

"You're fired!" Shankar exclaims, decommissioning me as navigator.

As we paddle closer to the city, the jungle dwindles, giving way to a charcoal gray, postnuclear landscape littered with blackened stumps and heaps of ashes. At the beginning of every growing season fires are lit around the cultivated fields, an ancient method of holding the jungle at bay. We soon discover that this bleak corridor of land abuts a manicured tea estate. We follow the high, sheer bank, looking for a place to land. After about a mile we dock at the end of a stone pier, a leftover from the days of the raj, when most traffic and commerce in Assam was routed along the river.

Beyond the stonework is a massive, rusted iron gate, thirty-five-feet long, that serves as a trellis for six different species of creeper. We discover a path leading into the heart of the tea estate and wander about the grounds, hoping to locate the main house. No workers seem to be around. After an hour of walking, we follow a path that cuts diagonally through the rows of bushes. It leads us back to the river, about a kilometer downstream from *Lahey-Lahey*. To our surprise there's another stone pier with a large workboat tied to it. As we approach, we can hear voices and the clanging of a bell.

"Maybe they'll share lunch with us," Shankar says, hastening ahead. We slow up when we spot five men with shovels, a gang of army engineers; the officer in charge levels his gaze at us.

"Halt! Stop right there."

Shankar volunteers a greeting. "Ahoy, we're river travelers. We were looking for the estate house and then we heard your bell. It's lunchtime and we thought . . ."

"Shut up," the officer commands, putting a hand on the butt of his pistol.

The men raise their shovels. Between the engineers and us is a mound of freshly turned earth topped by a flimsy bamboo cage. Shankar clears his throat and tries again, this time extending his hand in a friendly manner. The two of us move slowly toward the group. I stop for a moment, resting my fingers on the bamboo cage.

"Are you growing vegetables?" I ask.

The soldiers start yelling; two of them whack the earth with their shovels and curse me; the officer races over and screams in my face. "How dare you defile a grave!"

I cringe. The funeral rites aren't even over. The bell we mistook as a dinner call was meant to scare off devils. The cage protects the corpse of a comrade from wild dogs and vultures.

"Sorcerers! Go! Leave us . . . Leave him!"

We walk backward for twenty yards before turning and sprinting for *Lahey-Lahey,* with the soldiers' curses following.

Back at the boat, Shankar asks, "Are you carrying your charms? The ones you got in Tibet."

"Sikkim," I correct him. "Yes, they're in my pocket."

"Just checking."

Later in the afternoon we see a pair of boats angling across the river. Each has a crew of five, with two men poling and the others manning long sweeps. Amidships the boats carry large industrial drums. As our paths intersect, we realize that the men are friendly *doodwallahs,* or milkmen, and the drums are milk cans. We ask for their advice on the river currents, and they insist on piloting us into Dibrugarh.

"You are now our guests," the leader says, grabbing hold of the rail and pulling our boats together. We can't decline the offer without offending them.

"The firang must not paddle. You," the headman says, pointing at me, "you must sit in my boat next to me."

With *Lahey-Lahey* sandwiched between them, we head for Dibrugarh ghat. This is the first time I've seen *Lahey-Lahey* from another boat, and I'm impressed by how well she slips through the water.

"Beautiful," I say, my eyes running over her sleek profile.

"Small," the leader comments.

"Yes, but pretty. Very pretty. Look at her."

"Very small."

"But fast."

"Not fast. Small."

As the tempo of the rowers picks up, one of the men starts thumping a metal drum with a stick to establish a cadence. A poler in the other boat summons his deep bass to sing a traditional story of a fisherman who is attacked by a giant crocodile. Rising from the depths and capsizing his boat, the crocodile chomps off the fisherman's legs. The devout hero, fighting for dear life, calls on the gods for help.

"Ram is good. Ram is god," the other doodwallahs chorus.

The crocodile is about to swallow the rest of the fisherman when Ram intercedes, restores his legs, and endows him with the strength of a god. The fisherman grabs the thrashing reptile and flings it into deep space.

"Ram is good. Ram is god."

One of the rowers in our boat leads the next song, of a doodwallah who keeps the faith when all appears lost. All his cows have been devoured by a giant turtle, but unlike his neighbors, who have also lost their cattle, this pious milkman continues to praise god every morning.

"Brahma brings life. Brahma is life."

The other doodwallahs in the village wallow in self-pity, but not him; he shares what little he has and asks for nothing in return.

"Brahma brings life. Brahma is life."

Appearing as a swan one morning, Brahma rewards the milkman's faith with a blessed seed. He plants it, and overnight his fields are covered with rice.

"Brahma brings life. Brahma is life."

Before the grain ripens, the swan reappears and leads the doodwallah to the river, where he reels in terror; not more than a shadow's length away is the giant turtle, snapping its jaws. But he doesn't run. As the turtle charges, the swan drops a blade of grass into his hand; magically, it becomes a sword.

"Brahma brings life. Brahma is life."

For a while the battle see-saws, but the swan distracts the turtle at a critical moment and the sword is driven home. No blood flows; instead, a herd of cows springs from the wound.

"Brahma brings life. Brahma is life."

Other songs follow until we land at Dibrugarh ghat, where the doodwallahs hurry off to sell their milk. For two Polaroid pictures, a gang of teenagers agrees to watch our gear while we follow the milkmen and head into town. We're both hungry, and this may be our last chance for a few weeks to escape our own cooking.

Main street is bustling. New macadam is being laid. Impatient drivers yell out their windows and honk. People swarm about, moving at a brisk pace — until they see me: there's always enough time to gawk at a firang. Several youngsters boldly approach, and the bravest speaks up: "The only white men we know are on TV. Are you one of them?"

Before I can answer, they scatter, dashing into stores and teahouses along the street. I look around and see a hand signaling to me from a police car. I'm instructed to get in.

Shankar, my pal, takes a step backward, smiles, and says, "Good luck, dude. I'll see you in the restaurant up the block."

At the station the commandant of Special Branch has been expecting visitors. He has already poured a cup of tea for both me and Shankar. "Where is your friend?" he asks.

"He's eating. We're very hungry."

"This will not take long if your papers are in order."

I take a seat and sign the foreigners' book as the commandant disappears into another room with my passport. The other officers join him, leaving me alone in the main office. Several patrolmen walk into the station and look at me with surprise. I direct them to the back room. This goes on for almost fifteen minutes before I get up to see what's keeping the commandant.

"Something wrong?" I ask, poking my head into the room.

"No, just looking. We like these African seals. This is my favorite," the commandant says, fingering the great seal of Zaire in my passport. "I like this one," another policeman says, flipping the pages to the great seal of the People's Republic of the Congo.

"I'm hungry and tired, Sir . . ."

They let me go and I find Shankar in a restaurant. Plates of half-eaten food await me; he has already stuffed himself to the gills.

"Some friend," I say to Shankar. "Thanks a lot."

"The food is great . . . Try this first."

"No, I mean thanks for leaving me to deal with the police."

"My pleasure. Dig in."

We don't return to the boat until after sunset. The hustle and bustle of main street dies down at five, and it becomes a quiet, tree-lined avenue. Few cars are out and no one pesters me. At the ghat we join a group of boatmen gathered around a bonfire. Thick, oily smoke shrouds the firelight.

"The mosquitoes are as big as birds around here," one of the doodwallahs tells us. "The smoke keeps them away," he adds, pointing to a bucket of tar, a gob of which he tosses into the fire for our benefit. "The more smoke, the fewer bugs."

The milkmen have waited for us, hoping we'll follow them to their village on the opposite bank. We decline, content to stay here. We help them shove off. As they disappear into the darkness, we can hear their song long afterward.

"Brahma brings life. Brahma is life . . ."

More than a hundred people live on this mud flat. Our tent fits right into the neighborhood, the only difference being that our shelter houses two people, while the others house entire families. Only a few of these squatters depend on the river for their livelihood, the rest being idle farmers displaced from their land by the flood. As they wait for the government to make good on promises of flood relief, they're barely subsisting on the generosity of fishermen and ghat visitors like the doodwallahs.

Surprisingly, three people from Bangladesh are camped on the flats. They're off to one side, not welcome near the fire.

The Indians won't talk to them, but I do, and one old man tells me how he came to Dibrugarh by mistake. He paid a smuggler to transport him over the border into India and was put aboard a boat supposedly heading for Calcutta.

"I kept waiting and waiting for Calcutta. They forced me off at the last stop, here. Now I am farther from Calcutta than I was in Dhaka."

He begs during the day and sleeps under a piece of tar paper at night. I wonder how he managed to pay the smuggler in the first place.

"A foreigner like you dug deep into his pockets. He will see the glory of Allah. Will you?" he asks, holding out his beggar's bowl.

He sneers at my donation, saying, "You will never enter Allah's kingdom."

Around the bonfire people ask what we're doing at the ghat. Shankar tells them of our plan to paddle through Bangladesh to the sea. They shake their heads sadly. Three people say they will pray for us; one man points at my sneakers, saying, "You won't need those in a day or two. Can I have them now?"

As if on cue, the others chime in. Haven't we heard of the Nareesch gang? Don't we know that the dacoits have arms as thick as trees? Aren't we aware that the pirates can capsize a boat just by blowing on the water? Some fishermen tell how they were attacked and robbed in the Badlands. The skipper recounts the story as two of the crew act the dacoits.

"They sprang at us like tigers . . . They flew across the water. Their oars never touched the water . . . Such eyes! Devil eyes, like embers, burning holes . . ."

"Were you going upstream?" I ask the skipper.

"Yes, why?" he queries, huffing and puffing.

His answer bolsters my contention that the dacoits will leave us alone. I explain that it's much easier to attack a boat being poled against the current, and although vessels going downstream are usually laden with cargo, on the return trip, when the holds are empty, the pockets of the crew are full.

"Hah!" the skipper shouts. "The firang is a stupid firang."

Shankar announces our intention to leave at dawn, and the others now feel obliged to help their fellow Indian.

"Let the firang go by himself," one tells him, going on to describe in horrible detail the many ways in which the pirates can kill us.

An elderly sailor makes the most dire prediction of all, saying, "The dacoits will cut off your balls and use your scrotums for change purses."

Shankar returns to the tent while I stay behind to inquire about wildlife on the river. Once they tire of speculating about my future, I pass around the now wrinkled picture of the pink-headed duck. Once again no one has seen it, but the illustration sparks a heated debate on the best way to cook duck. Not much later I join Shankar.

In the morning, after paddling several miles downstream, we're back in duck country again. The jungle crawls over the riverbank; birds reappear; tracks along the shore mark the favorite watering spots for swamp deer, crab-eating mongooses, wild boar, and various species of cat. In one two-mile stretch, ducks carpet every foot of water; I figure there are 31,000 birds floating within sight.

"How did you come up with that?" Shankar asks.

"Math," I say authoritatively.

As we move through a flock of pochards, several pale red feathers drop from the sky and land near the stern. I keep a close watch on all the ducks and ready my cameras. Hundreds of storks are feeding in the shallows, clacking their mandibles. A crested serpent eagle eyes me from a treetop, and a chestnut-bellied nuthatch almost clips our rail as it races by, trying to tell me something important. I cock the camera shutter.

Slowly Shankar and I develop a perfect cadence, the rhythm of our paddles in harmony with the river. Our wake is imperceptible, barely hinting at our passing. The sun guides us downstream, marking the way with a slender golden path. We paddle on, our movement as fluid as the water itself. The sounds of the Brahmaputra have grown familiar, their clarity and intimacy comforting. As I listen, I begin to decipher pieces of the river's timeless message.

"Look out!" Shankar yells as *Lahey-Lahey* clears a bend.

I snap out of my trance to find that we're on a collision course with another boat. I back-paddle frantically, jabbing the water, trying to swing the bow around. Shankar is poised to fend off. The other crew, just as surprised, dig in their push poles. *Lahey-Lahey* misses their stern by inches and rounds up smartly, giving us the appearance of expert boatmen. She stops within an arm's length of their rail.

They're turtle catchers, and the two 150-pounders in their bilge indicate that they're good at their jobs. They were tracking a third when we appeared. The captain apologizes, explaining that they were focused on the bubble trail of their submerged prey. Shankar, wetting his lips at the thought of a turtle dinner, asks for the secrets of turtle hunting. The captain explains that there are two ways to catch a turtle: trapping it with a net or wounding it with a trident and roping it by the neck when it surfaces.

Turtles are the basis of his village's entire economy. The meat close to the shell is a delicacy that commands a high price in the city; the shell is carved into combs or decorative objects. The captain shows us some of his own handiwork, mostly combs, which, he notes, are of no use to me. They give us small amulets made from turtle shell, and in exchange we offer Michael Jackson lighters. Everyone is delighted with the barter.

Following the shifting main current, we cut all the way across the river to the north bank. When the wind is calm, it's relatively easy to plot the fastest course: ripples point us to the swiftest-running water. However, when it's blowing hard enough to put whitecaps on the waves, it's nearly impossible to track the current, and we must rely on luck.

Tonight it's my turn to cook. When Shankar goes off to collect firewood, I rifle through our supplies hoping for inspiration. By the time he returns, I've unpacked everything.

"What are you doing?" he asks, kindling the fire.

"Looking for something different."

As the fire catches, flames shooting through the top of the mustard oil tin, I can see the grin on his face. He knows we have plenty of food, but it's all the same. We end up eating rice, dal, onions, and radishes again, our standard menu, which varies only by the amount of curry powder or pepper we add. There was no tinned food for sale in Saikhoa Ghat; Moti explained that people won't buy food if they can't smell it or pinch it. Shankar decides to write out a shopping list of items to buy in the next town; he's still at it when I turn in.

Several uneventful days later, as we paddle between two large islands, Shankar yells, "Look at that." He's pointing to starboard, but I can't see anything. I raise my binoculars and scan the island. "Tiger?" I ask. Yesterday we spent the entire morning following the tracks of a Bengal tiger. We gave up after finding nothing but leeches.

"Forget the tiger. Look at the water. There!"

It's too late to avoid the whirlpool, so we hang on for the ride. It's the largest whirlpool we've seen, almost twice the length of the boat. Previously we've powered right through them, encountering little drag, but not this time. Around and around we go, spinning clockwise, making tighter, faster circles. The horizon becomes a dizzy blur.

"Yahoo!" Shankar exclaims, his paddle shipped, holding on to the painter like a rein. "Ride 'em, cowboy!"

This gleeful feeling is quickly supplanted by terror as the whirlpool starts to suck us down.

"Sheee-ittt. Paddle, paddle!" Shankar now screams.

Both of us thrust our oars into the swirling water as the foam starts lapping the gunwales. The boat lists, her port rail dipping under. The river pours in. We shift our weight to compensate, burying the starboard rail. *Lahey-Lahey* spins on her nose and threatens to dive. The bilge water surges forward, almost catapulting me from the stern. We stroke like madmen, shouting instructions at each other. Water cascades over the stem. We move aft, straining to regain an even keel. *Whap!* the stern hits the river. *Lahey-Lahey* corkscrews, reverses direction, and cuts across the spirals into calm water. We head for the nearest land.

Shankar and I had heard about these giant whirlpools, but we didn't believe the stories told us by Jodu Das, Hayna, and Moti. In Indian lore whirlpools are regarded as doorways to another life. An angry deity is lying at the bottom, sucking in the water, waiting to gobble some unwitting sailor to appease its wrath. The river gods may not forgive our next mistake.

We reach the right bank without further incident and discover a wide expanse of marshland. In a flash my mood changes.

"This is it, Shankar. We've found the perfect nesting ground for the pink-headed duck. Just look at that marsh."

Shankar is not excited; indeed, he groans as I steer for the wetlands. The air becomes thick with flying, biting insects, as well as a stomach-knotting odor of swamp gas. This doesn't deter me, for I sense that the duck is near. I jump out, eager to survey the area, but Shankar won't leave the boat. I point out a few of the highlights of this wonderland, including the thousands of iridescent dragonflies zipping over the stagnant water, flitting from one earthen mound to another, their bodies glistening like sapphires. Birds' nests are everywhere and the occupants shout their welcome.

"They're telling us to go away," Shankar corrects.

I remain undaunted, sure that the white ibis are grunting hello, that the chestnut bitterns are extending a gracious invitation, confident that the flapping widgeons and terns are applauding our arrival.

"I don't like it here," Shankar whines.

"Come on," I urge. "What's the problem?"

"It's just a feeling. I don't know . . . It's the kind of place a *burru* would live in."

"A what?"

"Burru. My grandmother told me stories about them. They're bad. Evil."

According to Shankar's grandmother, burrus appear in two forms, the most frightening being that of a giant, scaly ogre with the claws of a panther and the head of a frog; the more common variety, I'm told, looks like a brontosaurus. In either case the god-beast regards human beings as tasty hors d'oeuvres.

"She saw one and my cousin did too. I'm telling you the truth . . . Hey, man, don't mess with burrus."

"Ah, come on," I chide.

"Forget it. I'm not going with you . . . My grandmother wouldn't lie about something like that. She was too religious to make up a story about the gods."

His grandmother once saw a black beast moving swiftly along the edge of the river. At first she had no idea what it was, but when it raised its head above the treetops she knew it was a burru. She ran and hid, saying prayer after prayer. Like a python, the beast eats its dinner, usually an elephant, in one gulp. The earthen mounds in the marsh are its dung heaps, each containing the skeleton of a devoured animal.

"Those mounds are sacred," Shankar says, pointing into the marsh.

"Holy shit!"

"Cool it! This is no place for jokes. The area is taboo, man, taboo. Let's split."

"Give me thirty minutes?" I entreat.

Shankar consents, but he won't participate in my survey of the flora and fauna. I wade into the ankle-deep water and head for the widgeons. After a couple of yards I slip into a trench and plunge up to my neck in water, so I swim to one of the sacred mounds. The birds are shrieking horrifically. What happened to the sweet, inviting chirping? I leap for the next mound, miss, and fall flat on my face, mouth in the ooze.

"Had enough?" Shankar calls.

I'm about to concede when my legs start disappearing into the soft bottom. I recall this feeling from a trip up the Congo River years ago. Once the muck is over your knees, it's nearly impossible to get out. I grab frantically for the reeds and slowly inch out on my belly.

"Now I'm ready to go," I confess, spitting out mud.

"Ugh! Look at you. Leeches, leeches everywhere. Serves you right," Shankar rejoins.

We use cigarettes to burn them off. Shankar attacks those on my back while I go after the suckers in my armpits and crotch.

"Hold still. Don't move," Shankar advises, removing one from my left ear.

A mile farther on, near the mouth of a small tributary, we hear a loud splash. What was that? The answer arcs through the air: it's a Ganges dolphin. We ship the paddles and wait for it to reappear. The mammal is nearly seven feet long with a snout like a barracuda and dull black skin. Ganges dolphins differ from their salt-water cousins not only in appearance but also in behavior; neither playful nor gregarious, they surface only for air, exposing their tiny eyes and chiseled teeth.

Since leaving Dibrugarh, the turtle catchers are the only people we've encountered. But Shankar is quick to remind me that many people are probably watching us. We're in the middle of the Badlands.

"This is where that boat got robbed, don't you think? The captain said they were near the mouth of a small tributary," Shankar recalls, adding that the dacoits attacked him not far from here.

As the sky turns purple, we begin to search for a safe place to camp. We don't want to sleep on the shore, and the only islands we pass are too wet, barely a foot above water. We keep paddling, hoping to find other boats or a ghat not shown on the maps. After the incident in the whirlpool, we resolved not to travel at night. Yet here we are paddling by the light of a quarter moon, able to see only a few yards off the bow. Every time I'm ready to pitch the tent, Shankar finds something wrong with the place. When he wants to stop, I demand that we push on. We're both hungry and irritable, but our bickering ends when we sight a campfire. We paddle toward it cautiously, trying to be quiet, picking up speed as we discern the lines of a fishing boat, about fifty feet long, with a bluff bow and a wineglass stern. The massive rudder is made of a latticework of teak boards. On deck a fire dances above the lip of an oil drum hanging by davits. No one appears to be aboard.

"Hell-o . . . Hell-o. Can we come aboard? Hell-o . . ."

Silence. I shine my flashlight up the curve of the sheer to the deckhouse. The light catches the eyes of five men huddled in the shadows. I lower the beam and see three knives. I douse the light and we're about to paddle off when someone shouts in Bengali, "Go away."

"Phew," Shankar exhales in relief. He responds, "We're friends, not robbers. Look! Look at him." He takes the flashlight and shines it on my face. "A firang. He's a firang."

I hear the men gasp. Shankar continues, "We need a place to sleep."

They confer privately while we stand in our boat, holding on to their rail. One man keeps shaking his head. Finally a decision is made.

"You can come aboard . . . Leave your knives behind."

A crewman bends over the side and gives us a hand up. None of them has seen a westerner before, and the man helping me won't release his grip. Another crewman holds a kerosene lamp to my face, raising and lowering the wick as he moves the light.

"Hmmm," he muses, adding something Shankar doesn't

understand that causes the crew to explode with laughter. Whatever the joke, it breaks the tension.

"My name is Gopal. Welcome," says the captain. "We were ready to kill you. We thought you were dacoits."

I thank him for his restraint and present them with Michael Jackson lighters. The captain, wanting to reciprocate, motions for us to sit down. He scurries into the cabin and returns with a small paper bag.

"Dreams," he announces.

The fire is lowered from the davits and brought amidships, where we gather to talk. They're all from Lalgola, a town on the Ganges in West Bengal. Gopal, afflicted with a tubercular cough, is almost thirty years old; the others are in their teens or early twenties. All have thick, calloused hands. There are no winches or motors aboard; their arms alone pull in the 150-foot nets.

"This boat," Gopal declares proudly, "our home, was built in 1953, and it's still in good shape. My father helped build her . . . He was a good fisherman and we worked the Ganges together for years. I grew up on this boat."

The boat, made of teak, is double-planked below the water line. The mast is a debarked babul tree stepped far forward, like that on a catboat. However, it's used exclusively as a towing stanchion; no sail has ever been hanked to it. An arched roof of thatch, tin, and bamboo covers the foredeck; all fishing is done from the aft quarter, where the deck is flat and open. The boat's name is *Lucky*, but Gopal has often thought of changing it.

"Years ago my father and I were fishing. Just the two of us. I was asleep and when I got up, he was gone . . . My mother cried and cried. She said that is what happens to all fishermen. He heard the river calling to him."

Gopal assumed command at the age of seventeen, and for the first few years he was moderately successful. That was when the fish population of the Ganges was still thriving.

"But each year we caught less. Now there is nothing for the nets in the Ganges."

This is his second season on the Brahmaputra, and it may be his last. As an outsider working the Assamese waterways, he must pay the state a 40 percent tax on his catch. That's the law, anyway; the actual tariff may vary according to the official on duty.

"If Shiva is kind, the tax man will take only four of ten fish. Sometimes he takes six. We have no one to protect us. We are not Assamese, so no one listens to our complaints."

Sunal, a lanky man who should wear glasses but doesn't, recounts an incident from two weeks ago. They were fishing downstream and had brought their catch to Sibsagar market. The tax man took most of their fish.

"We went to the police and they told us to leave if we didn't like it here. The tax man is Assamese, the police are Assamese, and we are Bengalis. That is not good for us."

A hush comes over the boat when I ask about the river pirates. The dacoits have left them alone, but the fishermen are superstitious and are afraid that mentioning the dacoits will ruin their luck. Gopal does tell us that spies in the market tip off the dacoits, identifying which boat has delivered a rich load.

We've dipped into the dream bag three times, postponing dinner until everyone's stomach is growling. At Gopal's command the food is prepared. Lobas, the twelve-year-old cook and apprentice fisherman, takes charge. He greases the pots and reaches into the hold, pulling out five containers of spices: hot chili peppers, green peppers, black peppers, more chili peppers, and curry powder. He takes some of each pepper and pulverizes everything with a porcelain rolling pin.

"The juice," he confides, "you must get all the juice."

While the ingredients simmer in mustard oil, Lobas dices some potatoes as a special treat for us. He adds water and drops in seven small fish called *bhangnon-mas*. After bringing the pot to a boil, he adds two fistfuls of curry powder. A half hour later, when the rice is cooked, we wolf down the food.

"Delicious," I say to Lobas, who beams.

Slowly at first and then with numbing intensity, the spices release their power. I ask for the water bucket. My insides feel as if they're melting and dripping out through my pores.

"Ah, you really do like it," Lobas says, watching me down a quart of water.

In the morning *Lahey-Lahey* looks woefully small next to the high-sided fishing boat. The crew of the *Lucky* call our boat *Susek,* Bengali for dolphin, but Gopal is more critical: "It's no bigger than a Christian's coffin! May the gods smile on you . . . You paddle a toy."

With this encouragement, we bid farewell and head out into the morning mist, hoping to make Sibsagar before dark. Several hours later we near the spot where the dacoits had attacked Shankar. For the first time he recounts the details of that day.

"I was lost in those islands over there, next to the bank. I took the wrong turn and followed a stream that led to a sandbank. I saw this guy standing on the shore and asked for directions . . . When I got near him, he started running at me . . . Two more came out of hiding. Phew, I was lucky. I hit one with my paddle and jumped aboard. Then, man oh man, I rowed like crazy . . . The next morning I took the bus home."

The story gives me an idea, and I suggest that we pretend the dacoits are closing in for an attack. "How fast can we go?"

We stroke double-time, thrusting our paddles into the river, pulling as hard as we can. *Lahey-Lahey* surges forward. We pour it on and pull triple-time. The boat slices cleanly through the water, no longer staggering between strokes. In rapid fire our paddles punch the surface. *Whack! Whack! Whack!* Shadows barely keep up with us. Everything rushes by — the shoreline is a blur of jungle colors. Faster, I want to go faster. I feel invigorated by every stroke; all that matters is movement. One moment blends into another. Faster! Ever faster into the unknown. I feel the pink duck is nearby, hiding just beyond view.

"Whoa! Look at that!" Shankar exclaims, ending our sprint.

"Keep going. Faster!" I urge.

"Check it out, man. Ahead," he says, pointing to someone walking along the beach.

I snap back. "Sorry . . . oh, yeah, I see him."

Shankar takes the binoculars for a closer look. "Well, dude," he drawls, watching the lonely figure, "he looks like a genuine fisherman. I can see a net, but we keep going and stay away from the shore, right?"

Not noticing us, the man continues walking toward a giant bamboo wishbone with a net strung across it. The contraption is suspended between a pair of thirty-foot poles. He releases a line, sending the mesh down into the water. A few minutes later he grabs a length of jute and uses his body weight as a cantilever to raise the king-size scoop. As it climbs into the air, the net shimmers like a spider's web covered in dew. Slowly the thousands of water droplets fall away, each a prism releasing miniature rainbows. The trap is effective; he catches a half dozen fish while we watch.

Beyond him a herd of water buffalo drinks from the river. The large bulls wear iron bells that clang like buoys. On the bank above the herd a shack is perched perilously close to the edge. As we round a sharp bend below it, we surprise several women bathing. Even though they're wearing saris, they're embarrassed, and we try not to stare. A little farther on we moor *Lahey-Lahey* next to five other boats. A path angles up to the flimsy building we saw from the water. Above its entrance the word "Tea" is scrawled in white paint.

The owner of the teahouse is hastily sweeping the dirt floor. He saw us coming, but he's not quite ready.

"Just one minute more . . . Please be patient," he says.

"It looks fine. We don't care," I reply.

"You should care," the shopkeeper tells me. "Just a few more seconds . . ."

Finally he allows us to enter his neat shop. He tells his son to leave the cook fire and alert the village that a firang has arrived. We sit down just as the water comes to a boil. On the wall near the kettle are postcards of exotically colored Hindu saints in various coital positions.

"They look happy," I observe.

"And we know why," he says, rubbing his fingers inside two cups.

"Where are we?" Shankar asks.

The man thinks for a moment. "Ahhh, yes, Rupahimukh Ghat. That's it, Rupahimukh Ghat."

The village is not listed on my map. He sees my confusion and adds, "Kalitas Town. That's what we call it." That name isn't listed either.

"How many people live here?"

"Several hundred. It changes. Sometimes more, sometimes less. It all depends on the blessing of the gods," he says, eyeing my notebook suspiciously.

As we drink our tea, the little shack fills with villagers of all ages. We're especially honored when the Village Council appears. Every time I ask someone's name, the answer is the same: "Kalitas." In this remote village people share food, chores, and a name.

"We are all Kalitas. We come from Kalitas. Our children are Kalitas," Kalitas tells me.

"Don't you use initials?" I ask, remembering how the Gurkhas lessened the confusion.

"What for? We know everybody. I am Big Kalitas. Over there is my father, Old Kalitas, and there is my daughter, Baby Kalitas."

I take out my Polaroid and line up the Kalitas clan for a portrait. Pleased, Big Kalitas grabs my hand and leads me away from the teahouse.

"Come, you must meet Mother Kalitas."

Only half of the village buildings survived this year's flood, and those that are left bear scars from the deluge. The high-water mark on his house touches the eaves, and sections of plaster are missing from the façade, exposing the bamboo lathing. The left side looks as if the breeze is the only thing holding it up.

"We are starting to rebuild, but we have no money," Big Kalitas sighs. "Our cows are all gone, lost to the river. Look at our fields covered in sand. It will be a year before the next harvest . . . everything must be tilled three, four times."

Once we're inside the two-room house, villagers crowd around the openings, vying for a good look at us. Outside the back door I can hear the *splish-splash* of milk squirting into a metal bucket. Baby Kalitas stares at me with large black eyes. She giggles when I smile at her but recoils when I go to pick her up. Mother Kalitas stands nearby, ready to strike a match the second her husband lifts a cigarette.

"During the flood," our host tells us, "the government made us leave. They took us to the hills on buses. Hundreds of us, all from different villages, were kept like goats . . . They promised help when we came back. Since then one helicopter has come and unloaded six bags of barley. Six bags of barley!"

As the Village Council leader, this Kalitas must deal with the complaints of all Kalitases. "Sleep is something I want but don't get," he says wistfully. He's unsure whether relief will ever come.

"Several years ago a calf was born with two heads. That was a good sign, we thought the gods were pleased with us. But you know, when I think back, the calf never knew what it was doing. One head wanted to go right, the other left. It died after a couple of months."

Daughter Kalitas, a slender teenager, brings us a tray with two cups of fresh milk and a bowl containing bread and sugar, the traditional offering of hospitality. After eating, we're led to the village center, a vacant lot where the temple once stood. The elders sit in chairs, with the oldest at the head of the group. Two men come from a nearby house with instruments, and a holy man follows, carrying an urn of water. The musicians set up and begin playing cymbals and a *khol* (drum); Priest Kalitas chants, "Water cleanses, water creates, water redeems." He digs his heel in the sand. From the depression he scoops up a handful of dirt and tosses it into the air. "This is the earth. This is our home. May Shiva bless us all."

The music grows louder as the tempo increases. Our host asks us to stay, but with several hours of daylight remaining, we decide to push on. After we have shaken hands with all the villagers, an informal procession escorts us back to the river, led by the holy man. A young girl presents me with a bouquet of wildflowers, and I bend down to kiss her cheek. Shankar puts several of the blossoms in his hair, to the delight of the Kalitases. The cymbals sound farewell. As we move downstream, a figure bolts from the crowd and runs along the bank, waving and keeping pace with *Lahey-Lahey*. It's the girl who gave us the flowers.

12

Kali's Left Breast

BELOW KALITAS VILLAGE the Brahmaputra begins to narrow, shrinking from three miles to less than one. As the river funnels into the tighter channel, the current accelerates and hurries *Lahey-Lahey* along with it. We must be doing six or seven knots. Above us, flying in a V-formation, is a flock of mergansers. They descend, quacking loudly, curling the tips of their wings to spoil the air flow. Far downstream I spot a flock of teal, and a pariah kite climbs in the western sky.

As daylight fades, so does the hope of reaching Sibsagar before nightfall. We head for a ghat off the starboard bow, resigned to spending the night. A young boy is fishing from the shore; it's the first time we've seen anyone using a drop line.

"Catch anything?" I shout.

"Sometimes," he replies without raising his head.

"What do you use for bait?"

"It depends," he says as we coast by. He looks up then, and when he sees my face, the line drops from his hand.

"Don't worry," Shankar hollers, "he's a firang. That's what they look like."

We moor at the ghat, which we learn is called Salmora. Though it is known throughout the northeast for its pottery, Salmora is considered too small to be put on maps. The pots and urns made here are shipped down the river on large boats. We walk over to inspect these craft, which look like dismasted caravels with their high sterns, plunging bows, and ample tumble-homes. The boats are connected to the bank by a series of catwalks, and workers cross the narrow planks bearing heavy loads of pottery on their heads. The urns are separated into tiers by layers of straw and stacked in neat rows. Once the boat is full, it will head out, stopping at every market from here to Bangladesh; whatever doesn't sell is trucked on to Calcutta and Dhaka from there.

One of the workers shows us his favorite teahouse, just twenty yards away, where we meet Ramesh Bhorali, the owner of the establishment. He has the face of a cherub and walks with a nautical roll. He interprets my arrival as a good sign.

"Shiva blesses me. A firang. What fortune!" he says jubilantly, an unusual and very welcome reaction.

After filling us with sweets, he offers to lead us on a tour. The perimeter of the village is dotted with deep holes, not one of which is marked or roped off. People seem to dig these shafts wherever they please to get at the best clay, which is usually in a stratum four to eight feet below the surface.

Both men and women dig and make the pottery, but only members of the lowest castes throw the clay on a wheel; Brahmins pat and shape the clay over wooden forms. The uncured pots are painted with a red or black glaze and placed on an open stone platform above a firebox. As the last tier goes into place, logs are piled in the hearth. While the heat builds, the mound of pottery is covered with a thin mixture of mud and clay, forming a skin that retains the heat. The end result is an enormous mud mushroom. Steam and smoke escape through a vent in the crown.

"Once we forgot the hole," a fireman tells me. "A couple of hours later the whole thing exploded. Clay went all over the place . . . What a bang."

The most important factor in the firing is even distribution of heat. Throughout the twelve-hour process the firemen constantly touch the skin, gauging the temperature with their fingertips. If an area feels too hot, they pull away sections of the crust or dampen the vents on the fire doors. A full day after the fire is out, when everything has cooled, the skin is broken off and the pottery removed.

Ramesh sends his only employee off to capture some pigeons for a special meal in our honor. As word spreads about the firang, the small restaurant fills. I pass around my picture of the pink-headed duck and, unexpectedly, one man nods his head.

"Yes, I've seen it. The pink one comes to my bathing spot," Mohikanata Saikia tells me. "Whenever I take a bath, they seem to be there. Two of them . . . Come with me the next time."

"Tomorrow?" I ask excitedly.

"Next week."

"You will wash tomorrow, Mohikanata," Ramesh insists.

Mohikanata reluctantly agrees. "Maybe Tamuli can come with us. He knows all about ducks and birds and animals. I will find him."

Ten minutes stretch into an hour. All I can think about is the duck. People talk to me, but I can only pretend to listen. Finally Mohikanata returns with Tamuli, a tall, light-skinned man with an intense gaze, the village naturalist. He scrutinizes the picture and takes a seat. I order tea for him. I want to toast my good fortune.

"This is a very rare bird," Tamuli says. "My father taught me about them, but I have never seen one."

"Mohikanata says the gūlāb-sīr visits this area whenever he bathes."

"Impossible. No animal would go anywhere near Mohikanata until after he washes," he jokes before handing me back the picture and talking seriously. "I believe Mohikanata is confusing pink with red. There are lots of red pochards at this time of year."

"Are you sure?"

"I can't be positive, but I go to the river every day . . ."

Tamuli is a policeman, and whenever he's off duty, he wanders to the river to watch the birds or simply to sit and listen to the water. He attended Sibsagar College, but his most valuable lessons came from his father.

"He taught me about the river. He was the best guide in the district. No one could track animals like my father . . . He could identify a bird a hundred meters away.

Ramesh bangs a kettle and shouts, "Eat! Eat! Eat!" The delicious aroma of the pigeon stew has attracted so many people that we have to share bowls. Tamuli and I sit at one end of the table, talking about birds. He confides that one of his dreams is to take a trip to the Antarctic.

"I want to see the penguins."

After the meal, Ramesh, eager to continue the festivities, urges Tamuli to play his *paepa,* a high-pitched instrument made from the horn of a water buffalo. This inspires Mohikanata, who leaves to get his turtle-shell zither. The low, twangy plucking on the zither produces a sound complementary to the high range of the paepa. Ramesh brings out a khol and cymbals. The musicians move outside and begin playing traditional folk songs. The sound stirs the rest of the village awake. Soon the path leading to the ghat is lit by flashlights and kerosene lanterns as people head our way. Intoxicated by the rhythm, a half-dozen men begin dancing like dervishes. Three women join them, moving their hands and feet in a very sensual and inviting way. Two grandchildren prop up an elderly man as he shakes his legs. I'm pulled into the middle of the circle and try to match the steps of one young male dancer, but there doesn't seem to be a pattern, at least none that I can discern. Resorting to the "Swim," I create a favorable impression.

Behind us, near the boats, a fire builds into an inferno. The smell of incense wafts our way. Tamuli dedicates the next number to the soul of the man being cremated at the water's edge. He strikes a mournful dirge while a baritone sings to the gods. The drum pounds a slow, somber beat; the paepa wails; and the cymbals punctuate the end of each refrain. Afterward the dancing and music return to a feverish pitch, and the party continues well into the night.

Tamuli and I stay up to talk after the others have gone to sleep. On my maps he marks the best places to look for birds.

"To watch nature, you must never stare at an animal. Look off to the side and talk to it in a gentle voice, especially here," he says, pointing to a place downstream. "Please tell no one about it. This is a very special place."

In the morning Mohikanata agrees to make a paepa for Shankar. We watch him heat an iron poker to burn away the core of the buffalo horn. Mohikanata assures us it will take him only twenty or thirty minutes to finish the instrument, but three hours later we're still watching him. Over and over he heats the iron and sears the horn. The diameter of the opening must taper precisely to yield the correct sound. Once this is accomplished and the tone established, he burns six holes for the stops. Last comes the placement of a reed at the mouthpiece. Shankar, though far from proficient, impresses us with his first sounds, a squeaky rendition of "Three Blind Mice."

We shove off in the early afternoon laden with pottery. Ramesh sees us off. A photo I took of him dangles from his neck. Tamuli is on police duty, but he has left a note promising to contact me if he ever sees the duck. Enclosed in the envelope with the note is a small pebble, a good luck charm given to him by his father. I carefully place it in my bag of talismans.

It's a hot, lazy day, and we end up drifting more than paddling. Only the waterbugs seem to be in a hurry, skittering about on the ends of their long legs. No other boat is in sight. We stop periodically to collect plants, gathering a few rare but well-documented species. To supplement our medical kit, I stock up on *Cymbidium giganteum,* a showy orchid with leaves that help clot blood. As we draw abreast of Sibsagar, neither of us is inclined to disrupt the placid afternoon by visiting a city. We float by with the current, keeping to the north shore, and eventually camp on an unremarkable island with one tree.

That night I dream I'm a bird, the wind lashing my face as I race over the river. I spot the silhouette of a fish in the water and dive for it. *Splash!* The water cradles my body as I plunge. My form changes and scales appear; a tail develops; my gills strain for air. I can suddenly turn, dart, hover, or glide. I swim to a sunken canoe with half its planking rotted away. A school of small fish live in the stern, and I ask them about the pink-headed duck. Yes, they've just seen it and wonder how I could have missed it. Minutes ago one was dabbling along the far shore. I'm off, cutting across the river, wending my way through the islands. At the shore I crawl up the bank like a salamander and slowly regain my human form. I awake with a start, my body chilled. The campfire is out, Shankar is snoring, and the river droning. Falling back asleep is easy; I'm learning where to look for nature's prize.

The next morning I inspect every flock we pass, looking for the pink duck. Twice I spot a misfit among the widgeons, but the duck doesn't sparkle pink when it turns in the sunlight. The wildlife thins as we approach the densely populated eastern tip of Majuli Island, the world's largest river island, sacred to all Hindus, and headquarters to several reformist sects.

According to Indian myth, eons ago an enraged Kali was destroying the earth during a tantrum. To save mankind Vishnu threw his iron discus, the wheel of death, chopping the goddess into many small parts. Shiva, Kali's grieving consort, gathered her remains and flew skyward, scattering her radiant body as he went and thus forming the constellations. Fifty-one pieces of the goddess fell back to earth. Majuli Island, remarkable in size, was her left breast. For as long as anyone can remember, pilgrims have been coming here to pay homage to Shiva and Kali.

We pull up to the island's ghat, where a teenaged boy insists on helping us drag *Lahey-Lahey* ashore. We go about our work, ignoring him as he tries to convince us of his worth as a guide. A voice cackles above us; it's a man waving from the upper deck of a large workboat owned by the state. Narayan Dutta, the caretaker, invites us aboard and gives us tea. While we sip the strong brew, he entertains us with tales of Majuli, its sights and history. At one point he stops in midsentence to look at his watch: the bus to town leaves in a few minutes and there isn't another one for three hours. Shankar and I sprint off to catch the bus, agreeing to meet Narayan for dinner. For the entire five-mile trip to town over scrub and sand dunes, we see the damage from this year's flood. Water buffalo and cattle scrape the sandy fields, scrounging for food. They look painfully thin.

We head directly for Na Satra, a famous religious commune near the center of town. Walking next to us, matching our stride, is a young novitiate dressed in white. We strike up a conversation, and within a couple of minutes Puspa has appointed himself our guide. As we walk, he tells us that bhakti, his cult of Hinduism, rejects castes and idol worship in favor of a more humanistic, personalized approach.

"We speak directly to the creative forces . . . We concentrate on life as we see it in our hearts. You will not find statues or idols here."

Because Hinduism is more a way of life than a religion of doctrines, Na Satra strives to recreate the ideal way of life.

"We are very strict in our observance of prayer and good works. There are no castes, no privileges in Na Satra. We live as brothers . . . It is a simple life."

The grounds, encompassing several hundred carefully tended acres, are impressive. At the center sits the main temple, an intricate wooden structure with a vaulted ceiling supported by a complex system of joists and rafters. Ringing the interior is a chair rail; the wall is painted white above the rail and green below. The floor is smooth, hard-packed dirt. Following us at a distance, a limping man sweeps away our footprints with a small broom. At one end of the temple a raised platform supports an altar and a lectern. An ancient backdrop of silk hangs from the rafters. Once an image was painted on the cloth, but the golden colors have faded. Moth holes perforate the silk; I touch the border and a piece of it crumbles into dust.

"Please, don't do that," Puspa admonishes.

A bell tolls and Puspa turns to face the south. For the next couple of minutes we stand silently as he recites his afternoon prayers. He explains that the bell chimes fourteen times a day, reminding the community to offer themselves to god. The routine changes on Tuesday nights, when Na Satra hosts a dance and concert. I've yet to see any women in the compound.

"Women may come to our dances," he says, pursing his lips, as if there's a sour taste in his mouth.

When I prod him for more information, it slowly comes out that he and the other 160 males living here equate women with temptation. If Na Satra were not dedicated to preserving the ancient Assamese folk music and dances, Puspa thinks women would not be allowed to enter the commune gate.

"We have become a center for Assamese folk traditions and we will oblige our role . . . Anyway, it is only one day a week."

Radiating out from the temple are narrow avenues crowded with houses identical in shape and size. Six to eight men live as a family unit in each one, with two elders acting as parents.

"We are grouped according to age. Each house has someone under ten. Then there is a teenager, someone in his twenties, another in his thirties . . ."

Puspa, now in his early twenties, entered the commune at the age of seven. There are two new members in his house.

"One of my fathers died," he explains. Longevity appears to be one of the benefits of this monastic lifestyle, for his father lived to a ripe age. Puspa assures me that "prayer extends life in all ways."

The community is virtually self-sufficient. The members grow their own food and generate income through the sale of musical instruments and fees charged to pilgrims on retreat. As we walk back to the main gate, I notice the man with the broom entering a small door at the back of the temple. He stops at the threshold to bow. Curious, I wander over. The room is separated from the rest of the temple by a plaster wall. Several idols smeared with red dye are arranged near one corner. The largest sculpture depicts an unearthly creature with the body of a lion and the head of a doe.

Puspa is quick to explain: "We don't pray to them. They are very old and valuable, so we store them here . . . What else can we do?"

Back in town, a three-block strip of restaurants and boardinghouses, we hire a jeep to take us to the other, more famous Satra commune. Founded in 1740 and supported by Ahom kings until the British seized control, Aunia Ati Satra is twice the size of its cousin. Two middle-aged men walk us through the complex. It's similar to Na Satra, but on a much grander scale. The grounds are expansive, the housing extends down long shaded avenues, the temple climbs to the sky; even the bell summoning the faithful is bigger.

We're taken to meet the elders, who salute us in the traditional Satra fashion: with palms together, they touch their chins and slowly nod, their eyes shut. Two young boys bring out a tray laden with flattened rice, yogurt, sugar, bread, and areca nut, a menu reserved for formal occasions. The old men smile but are silent, lifting their eyes heavenward at each of my questions. A gong sounds and everyone leaves the room; not sure what to do, Shankar and I follow.

"The master awaits you. Come," someone finally says.

Mukhya, the sect leader, is about sixty years old, and extremely cross-eyed. Frozen in the lotus position, he takes his time before speaking. He's barefoot, clean-shaven, and wearing a spotless white outfit. His spooky eyes hold my attention.

After greeting us, he declares in a low, unnerving voice, "I can see into you and beyond you. I have the power of the third eye."

Not willing to challenge this assertion, I shift my gaze to his arthritic hands. I naively ask the master to explain the teachings of the satra. He does so, and in less than ten seconds, I'm totally lost. He rambles on nonstop, jumping between the past and the present, detailing life five hundred years ago in the same sentence as life today. He remembers his former lives clearly; they are part of his conscious past, echoing his future. Eventually he ends his monologue and asks if we have any more questions.

"No, Holiness," I respond, still reeling from his first answer.

"Good," he says and claps his hands.

A young boy hurries to Mukhya's side for instructions. He leaves and returns carrying three volumes, each the size of a doorstop, of Mukhya's biography of Aunia Ati leaders.

"I have put it all down . . . all my lives are here, all the lives of the other masters are written inside this book. You must buy it to learn about us."

Besides being written in a language I can't read, the books carry a hefty price. Neither Shankar nor I offers to buy the set, so Mukhya resolutely starts to read aloud. Shankar gathers his courage and interrupts him halfway through the second page.

"Holy One, what is the story of the tulsi tree?"

Mukhya closes his skewed eyes and explains that the story of the log is based on a dream he had many years ago. This surprises Shankar, who mentions that his grandmother once told him the tale and ascribed it to seers who lived centuries before Mukhya.

"It does not matter. Believe me or your grandmother." He glares at Shankar. "A tulsi log will someday float down the river growing two shoots that look like eyes. When this happens, god will follow, descending to earth. Often this log is reported, but I tell you it does not exist. The story came from my dream. That is all."

He invites us to stay and share their communal life. We decline and ask if we can take his picture before leaving. He grants our request, but not before he straightens his tunic and combs his hair. As I focus, he crosses his eyes even more than usual. Afterward he gives a blessing, wishing us "goodness."

Near the main gate a ghostly hand beckons from inside one of the enormous columns. A Shivaite, Saa Baba, has been given shelter inside the pillar. His skinny body is smeared with ashes, a scraggly beard reaches to his navel, and his tangled hair brushes the backs of his knees. He has been living in the column for two months and expects to stay another month before continuing on his pilgrimage to Benares. A walking stick is propped in one corner, and incense saturates the dank cubicle. I offer him alms, but he refuses.

"I asked you to visit me," he says touching my arm gently. "I wanted to see the firang . . . I want to give you a gift," he adds, handing us each an orange. "Think of Shiva as you taste the sweet juice."

We return to the ghat to find Narayan inspecting a cook pot. Sweat drips from his face, and he uses a finger to flick it back into the stew.

"Perfect. Just in time for dinner," he says triumphantly.

"What's cooking?"

"Fish stew. I hope you like it spicy."

I look around for my water bottle. While we eat the fiery stew, Narayan shares his impressions of the Satra communes. Like us, he finds Na Satra a pleasant place; he especially likes to go to their dances. The Aunia Satra, however, is a mystery to him.

"Did you see him? Did you see his eyes?"

Whatever reservations we have about Mukhya aren't shared by the thousands of pilgrims who flock to the commune, some staying as long as three months. Narayan tells us of the miraculous powers attributed to Mukhya, recounting stories told to him by the faithful. One man said Mukhya healed his blindness, another swore his cancer disappeared, and others talked of similar incredible cures.

"He has great power," Narayan insists.

Although this island is dedicated to the bosom of Kali, I've been unable to locate a single statue or reproduction of it. Narayan says there are none that he knows of: "This is not Kamakyha with all its poles and holes."

We cast off before dawn the next day, striking a course for the southern bank. The fog is once again thick, and within an hour we're lost in a maze of tiny islands. The keel scrapes mud, forcing us overboard to tow *Lahey-Lahey.* At one point we even drag her across an island, hoping for a shortcut to the main stream. It's exhausting work, and we heap abuse on each other. Considering that we've been together for more than two weeks, never apart longer than fifty minutes, I find it remarkable that Shankar and I are still talking.

Eventually we find deep water and plenty of river traffic. Downstream three boats are being towed against the current by crewmen on the bluff. Wherever possible, the crew abandons its poles for the tow line. The captain sits and steers while the others trudge along, singing in cadence, pulling the vessel upriver.

We pass Jorhat, the tea capital of Assam. Its large fishing fleet is on the water today; the boats work in pairs, with one craft anchoring the shore end of the net while the other heads midstream, the crew paying out the mesh as they go. The men from the beached skiff take positions about one hundred yards away and start wading through the shallow water, beating its surface with sticks and yelling. This signals the offshore boat to start circling back in, closing the trap. We watch the fishermen come up empty five times in a row. As Gopal told me several days ago aboard the *Lucky*, "You get used to coming up empty. This is India, you know."

A couple of days later, when we're camped several miles upstream from Kaziranga Wildlife Sanctuary, thieves strike. We normally sleep with our gear next to the tent, leaving only a few items in the boat, but that night our campsite is less than ten yards from *Lahey-Lahey* and we don't unpack everything. We sleep through the night, undisturbed, but upon awakening, we discover that our tools, pots, fishing tackle, and some clothes have been taken, and most unfortunately, Shankar's shoes.

"I'll get those bastards. I'll make them pay, man oh man, I'll get them," Shankar fumes.

"Forget it. We can replace everything . . . It was only a pair of shoes."

"Dogface, don't tell me it was only a pair of shoes. They were mine. I loved them."

"Let it slide."

Shankar finally quiets down as we come alongside the wildlife sanctuary. Kaziranga Park, a 165-square mile tract, borders the Brahmaputra for nearly twenty-five miles, more than a day of paddling aboard *Lahey-Lahey*. Along with the Manas Wildlife Refuge across the river near Bhutan, Kaziranga is the premier spot in India to observe big game, including the largest herd of one-horned rhinoceros *(Rhinoceros unicornis)* in Asia. Cats, monkeys, boar, deer, and hundreds of other exotic animals are found here. Our cameras hang at the ready as we paddle by this stretch of jungle.

Before 1900 the fabled rhinos were found in many sections of India, but now they are close to extinction. By far the single greatest threat is poachers coveting their valuable horn. For centuries people have attributed fantastic medicinal and aphrodisiac properties to powdered rhino horn. Supposedly a pinch of it can cure lethargy, cancer, or the common cold. Many of the lucky who own a horn rent them out; its presence under a bed is believed to ensure sexual potency, minimize the pain of childbirth, and drive the devil out of a sick person.

Anxious to see the menagerie, we paddle noiselessly, deftly sliding *Lahey-Lahey* along the glassy river. But not one animal comes into view. In fact, we even miss Kaziranga Lodge, where we had hoped to spend the night. Tucked behind a large sandbar, the colonial structure is hidden from anyone traveling downstream at water level. I spot it too late, while looking back over my shoulder. We decide to press on rather than pole against the current.

Our luck changes several miles later. We see a fishing cat crouched on an overhang with every muscle tensed, ready to spring. We drift in for a closer look at this rare feline. The wind, luckily, is off the bow and carries our scent away from the cat. As we near, I admire its silver-gray coat flecked with black spots. Its eyes are fixed on the water, its ears twitching. The cat has a reputation for killing cattle and dragging off dogs and babies. Shankar snaps a picture, and the click of the shutter breaks the silence. Startled, the cat spins and in one smooth motion bolts into the jungle.

Not far beyond, maybe a kilometer at most, we sight five elephants splashing in the river. They make a tremendous noise, one bull in particular bellowing its enormous presence.

"Give them plenty of room, Shankar. The bull is in musth. Look at all that black crud around his eyes."

Musth is the external manifestation of a year's worth of internalized rage, and for several weeks each year, a bull in musth is to be treated with extreme caution. Right now there's nothing predictable about him save his ferocity and ill temper. As we pass far to port, the elephant raises his trunk and blares at us. Just to make certain we know who's boss, he trumpets again, watching us until we disappear around the bend.

The air is exceptionally clear today. One hundred and ten

miles to the north the Se-La region of the eastern Himalayas is visible; the mountain peaks appear to be holding up one end of the sky. I think of the water flowing all the way down from the 23,000-foot Mount Chomo (Adorable Woman) to this spot under *Lahey-Lahey*. Near Chomo from our angle is Mount Kangto (Snow Giant), purportedly the second favorite child (Ganges being closest to his heart) of the Father of All Mountains and King of the Snow, Lord Himalaya. South of the river and to the east lie the low Mikir Hills, which once, eons ago, towered over the Himalayas.

According to Assamese folklore, the Brahmaputra was the issue of a forbidden love. From his home atop Mount Kailas, Brahma was entranced by the grace and beauty of Amogha, the mortal wife of an Assamese king. One day the king went on a pilgrimage and Brahma flew to the side of Amogha. He assumed the form of a goose and followed her about. As she bathed, the god became so excited that he climaxed, spilling a puddle of semen. When the king returned, he noticed the milky liquid and ordered his wife to drink it. Reluctantly she obeyed. Divinely impregnated, she gave birth to a son in the form of water. Water cascaded from her womb for weeks, creating a lake in the Himalayas. Growing ever larger, the lake became a sea, and its mass eventually split a mountain in half, springing the Brahmaputra on its holy course.

In Salmora we were told to report to the Kaziranga Park police, which we have failed to do. Not wanting to be mistaken for poachers, we shoot across the river to look for a remote campsite. We find one and settle into our evening routine.

"What are you doing?" Shankar asks as I open the bags of rice and dal.

"Dinner."

"Where did you find the pots? With my shoes?"

I have forgotten about the theft, but my brooding pal hasn't. After a meal of cookies and cigarettes, I leave Shankar at camp and set out for an evening stroll. The jungle, a factory of sounds, is less than a mile away, but this sparsely covered island is fairly quiet. Where reeds grow, crickets sing their mating calls. Croaking frogs flop into the water as I approach. Occasionally I hear the clicking of beetles, and twice the mournful cry of a brown fishing owl stops me. It's an eerie sound, hollow and long: "Habooom-ooo-habooom." To a superstitious Hindu two screeches of an owl presage success in an undertaking, whereas one is an omen of death. As the chill of night begins to penetrate, I return to the crackling fire, feeding it more thatch and bamboo. I shake my charms and think about the pink duck, hoping that the owl hoots herald a face-to-face encounter.

The next day, countless paddle strokes later, near the town of Bishnath, we spot some large rock formations where the Mikir Hills dip to the river, supplanting the alluvial plain with a craggy, forested landscape. The Brahmaputra traces a major geological fault line running between the Himalayas and the Mikir and Naga hills. Earthquakes are relatively common, and devastating ones occur approximately once every thirty years. The worst quake in recent memory (1950) nearly flattened Shillong, turning to dust several centuries of civilization. In one spot near Goalpara, the river channel shifted almost a kilometer to the south. Violent upheavals in the lower Brahmaputra dumped thousands of acres into the river, choking the stream and raising the level of the bed. The water, temporarily dammed, backed up and ploughed east-northeast, its flow completely reversed. Waves ten to twelve feet high marched upstream, destroying fishing fleets and washing away entire villages.

The town of Bishnath miraculously escaped major destruction. According to local lore, it was saved because of its numerous temples. From *Lahey-Lahey* we first see Bishnath as an elegant array of curved eaves and high domes floating above a rocky shore of mica and feldspar. The silicates reflect the light, making every crag and rock face sparkle. Bougainvilleas are in bloom, and lime trees sag under the weight of fruit.

Several fountains spew mist into the air. As we get closer, we begin to discern dark colors from shadows, and we note that most of the doorways are painted rich greens, blues, and browns. The lighter hues emerge slowly.

The town has an actual harbor, the first we've seen, its entrance marked by a twenty-five-foot stone obelisk. Two rusty hooks are attached to its tip; when Bishnath was a major port for British steamships, oil lamps were hung from the hooks to guide the night traffic. We beach just as a herd of water buffalo are driven onto the sand for their daily bath. After squeezing through the herd, we find ourselves at the beginning of a peaceful, shady street. Freshly whitewashed houses run the length of the avenue. It looks like a movie set, spared from the poverty and hardships affecting most other villages. Although no one is in sight, sounds of life abound: hammering, crying babies, clanking pots and pans. We stop at the first teahouse along the way.

The owner is out, but his son greets us like long-lost brothers. Makul hugs me with a wrestler's grip.

"How did you arrive? The bus is not due for hours."

"By boat."

"From where?"

"Saikhoa Ghat."

"Where's that?"

"Across from Sadiya. Up north."

"Impossible," he exclaims. "Too far away . . . Crocodiles — what about all the crocodiles?" He's disappointed to hear that we didn't see any, but he keeps staring at me as if something's nagging at him. Finally, after tea and sweet cakes, he whispers, "Did you see a burru?"

"No burrus, no crocodiles."

"Then what is wrong with your skin?"

"I'm an American and . . ."

"An American!" he says excitedly. "Wait, please. I must get something from home."

He comes back with an old cassette player and one tape, a

bootleg recording of Jethro Tull. Makul pops on the heavy-breathing flutist.

"My father forbids this music," Makul ruefully tells me.

"Why?"

"I think he got tired of it. Please teach me the words."

I sympathize with Makul's father; after the first cut, I, too, want to erase the tape. Midway through the recording, during a long instrumental, I ask Makul to turn down the volume, explaining that what he thought were words are only unintelligible grunts. I pull out the illustration of the pink-headed duck. He shakes his head and admits that he knows nothing about birds.

"But Atul does," he says, sending his baby brother off to fetch his pal. We drink tea as his other friends start arriving, having already heard about us through the Bishnath grapevine. Atul rolls up on his bike with several other friends, all of whom are trying to grow mustaches, only three with any success. Atul studies the picture. Like Tamuli, he has heard of the pink-headed duck but has never seen one.

"I was told you were looking for a bird. I thought maybe it was the white-winged wood duck. There are some around here."

"Where?" I ask. This is exciting news: the wood duck is the *second* rarest duck in India.

"In the marsh west of town, about two or three hours walk," he says. "Listen for this call: *Quack-a-quick-a-quack.*"

His imitation pleases me. At last I've met a quacking peer. Together we fill the teahouse with rare sounds.

"OK, cut it out!" Shankar shouts, threatening to play his paepa or more Jethro Tull if we continue.

Makul leads all nine of us on a bicycle tour of the city. The first stop is the market, where Shankar buys some shoes and I restock the kitchen and the tool chest. From there we head north on a gravel road leading to an ornate temple archway, on which are chiseled the many and various reincarnations of Shiva. We climb forty-one steps to reach the thirteenth-century shrine. The grounds are filled with animals. Chickens, goats, cows, monkeys, and deer wander freely; only dogs are chased away by the ever-vigilant priests. Most of the animals are streaked with yellow or red dye identifying them as living sacrifices. Years ago the faithful would buy an animal from the priests for sacrificial slaughter, but in the 1950s, bloodless sacrifice replaced the old method. A devotee tells me that the message of nonviolence preached by the Mahatma changed everything.

"Don't believe that," Makul whispers. "They changed for other reasons. Money. Now you buy life for an animal. The bigger the beast, the higher the cost."

I don't quite understand, and he tells me to touch the goat nuzzling my leg. Some of the dye rubs off on my hand.

"Now do you understand?" he asks. "It's a trick. Once the dye wears off, the priests resell the animal to another pilgrim. After the monsoon, every animal is for sale."

"Is that bad?"

"Some people still believe that blood is the only way to get the attention of the gods. At Kamakyha they still chop off heads."

The pre-Ahom architecture of the temple is a reminder that the area has Mongol, not Persian, roots. Constructed of stone covered with smooth red stucco, the temples of Bishnath are studies in classical proportion, and this Shiva temple is a fine example. Typically there are three basic design elements: a long, narrow entrance corridor, a circular main chamber, and a high domed roof.

"We come from the womb, enter the circle of life, and stretch for the heavens above us," Atul says, explaining the design.

I tie my shoes to a branch, out of reach of the goats, and enter the dark corridor. My head bumps the ceiling and my elbows scrape the walls. The dirt floor is damp and mossy.

Occasionally I step on something long and squishy. The ceiling lowers with every step, forcing me to crouch. All is black. Suddenly, although I can't see a thing, I sense that I'm in an open space, a tremendous void.

"Life begins," Atul says.

"Yes, it does," replies a strange voice. "May Shiva bless you and your children."

A match flares. The teeth of a priest gleam in the yellowish light. He ignites a torch, dispersing the Cimmerian darkness. The smoke curls upward, lingering in the peak of the dome. The priest approaches me. One of his hands is open, and his fingers look large and mutated. As he nears, I realize that he's actually holding out a fistful of candles. I make an offering of a ten-rupee note and he lights one and passes it to me. When no one else buys, he harumphs loudly and leaves.

Shankar tries to speak softly, but his voice is amplified by the acoustics of the stone chamber.

"That's why the temple is so sacred," Makul tells us. "In here you don't have to speak. The sound of the heart is as loud as thunder. The gods are sure to hear you."

Losing no time, I begin reciting a litany of wishes. Soon we're all asking for cars, cash, and CD players. As we chant, I notice that the walls hold a series of recesses, each a small altar housing a sculpture of Shiva. Like the Stations of the Cross, these icons depict Shiva's suffering for the benefit of mankind. Makul visits each shrine. His meditations change his mood, and he chides us for our material desires.

"What should we be asking for?" Shankar asks.

"Peace, love . . . things like that."

"Makul, do what you have to do. I need a CD player."

Having spent our wishes, we form a line and squeeze back into the tunnel. I extinguish the candle after the first few steps, not wanting to know what we're stepping in. At the door I spring out, stand tall, and gulp the fresh air.

"May Shiva bless you," says the priest who is waiting for us.

He extends his hand toward me, but not to shake. "The candle, please," he says, grabbing it.

We bicycle around for a few hours, visiting the public squares and ruins. Before the Ahoms migrated here in the thirteenth century from the north and east, Assam was the stronghold of Bodo tribesmen. Most of the place names come from the Bodo language, but little is known about the ancient culture. Rain, humidity, recurrent floods, jungle vines, and acidic soil have conspired against the cultural legacies, indiscriminately destroying temples and palaces. Few written records have survived the climate, though recently a trove of sitsal tree leaves enscribed with Bodo civil laws was found. Atul speculates that it may take years before they're deciphered.

"In Assam everything is lahey-lahey," he says, raising a smile from Shankar. Atul doesn't know the name of our boat.

During the tour Makul constantly asks us to close our eyes and imagine various grandiose structures. It's hard for me to do, as all that is left is a few ordinary-looking stones scattered about. After we visit the third site of possible ruins, two boulders in the middle of a rice paddy, Makul obliges my request to head back. I'm eager to return to the river. I can't put the white-winged wood duck out of my thoughts, and Shankar is anxious to use the waterproof marker in my kit to sign his name on his new sneakers.

"No one will ever steal my shoes again," he promises.

Makul helps us shove off, but when we're fifty yards off shore, easing into our paddling rhythm, an unfamiliar voice hails us. On the beach is a crowd headed by four policemen. We turn back, and the captain of the guard demands our papers. His men inspect our bags and make us empty our pockets.

"What's wrong?" Shankar asks.

The officer stands silently until his men finish their search. Sheepishly he confesses that he was forced to detain us because several citizens came to the station with reports of foreign agents: "Two Chinese spies on bicycles taking pictures." He points to the Village Council members standing off to one side and clicks his tongue. "One of them said you were carrying a shortwave radio."

We resume the voyage and keep a weather eye out for the white-winged wood duck. Atul described the marsh in detail, but he has never approached it from the water. At day's end we haven't spotted anything but sand, bush, and common waterfowl.

We join a camp of friendly fishermen, only two of whom have all their fingers. None of them has ever heard of Saikhoa Ghat or Sadiya, nor do they care to learn about them. They're homesick for Bihar, and as far as they're concerned, the less said about Assam the better. They fish only at night, using lanterns to attract their prey.

"The fish love the glow of the full moon. We fool them with our lamps," says their leader, Ramanand Mandal.

"Does it work?" I ask.

His eyes grow sad. Last year, after paying taxes and bribes, each of his men was left with thirty-eight dollars for seven months' work; he took home forty-five dollars. His list of woes is as long as a telephone book, and he appears happy only when detailing them. He believes someone has jinxed him, but he doesn't know who, or why they cast the spell. To lighten his load, I tell him the history of the Bodhi Tree and present him with a sliver. Before we part in the morning, he shows me the night's catch. It's the best of the month and he gives us two prize fish.

"Are you sure you got Atul's directions right?" Shankar asks several hours later. We've yet to sight a marsh.

"Positive."

"Sorry, pal, we missed it. Check it out up ahead. See the towers?"

Directly off the starboard bow is the outline of the Tezpur

bridge. From this distance it shimmers like a mirage: one instant it's clear, with its girders and trestles easily visible, the next it's an iron-red smudge. Even though tens of millions of people live along the Brahmaputra in Assam and Bangladesh, only two bridges span it, one in Gauhati and the other here in Tezpur. Because of the monsoons, the earthquakes, and the fantastic volume of water, the Brahmaputra presents a most difficult obstacle to engineers. When the Gauhati bridge opened less than thirty years ago, it was hailed as a remarkable feat; the Tezpur bridge, recently opened to traffic but not fully completed, was heralded at the ribbon-cutting ceremony as "one of the greatest achievements in history." The accolade is lost on the fishermen and boat crews working the river. To them it's a navigational hazard and a dyspeptic to the gods. Ramanand cursed the bridge; he wanted to see it blown into a million pieces.

"The people who built the bridge will be on their knees asking Brahma to forgive them. Never, my friend, never think that you can conquer god."

As we near the confluence with the Bhareli River, about fifteen miles upriver from the bridge, Ganges dolphins start popping out of the river again. It seems that the more turbid the water, the more dolphins we see. The silt from the Bhareli has formed long sandbars and dozens of small islets.

"Whoa! Turn her to starboard, Shankar."

In an inlet bounded by reeds and mud flats, a flock of red pochards appears, some preening themselves, others dabbling contentedly in the calm water. Off to one side, bobbing by themselves, are a pair of ducks bigger than the rest and different in color from the pochards. They have bright orange bills, white heads, and the coal-black bodies of wood ducks. We land and creep silently over the sandbar. The birds are less than thirty yards away. I can see a thin white line marking the crease of their folded wings. Perfect. We inch forward to get a good picture of the rare white-winged wood duck, which may soon be as scarce as its pink cousin.

"Oh, shit," I yell, leaping up, tossing my cameras to Shankar, and dashing toward the water.

It's my duty to secure *Lahey-Lahey* whenever we stop. As usual, I staked the push pole into the mud, but for some reason I never attached the painter. Shankar watches the marsh empty of birds as I splash into the river and swim for the drifting boat. I nearly capsize it climbing aboard.

"That was intelligent," Shankar says. "You blew the picture of the wood duck."

"Then it *was* a white-winged wood duck!"

"Hey, Sherlock, you're the bird nut. You tell me."

"Right," I say, taking out the log and writing, "Positive sighting of white-winged wood duck . . ."

Gradually the various sections of the bridge come together in our view to create a whole that gets bigger and bigger as we approach. Sentries stand watch high above us, studying our movements through field glasses. We wave and they return the gesture. If we had our cameras out, we would probably be arrested. Photographs are prohibited anywhere near Indian bridges, railway stations, or airports. Officials look the other way when a tourist snaps an old structure like the Delhi railway depot, but around new projects the law is strictly enforced. As Ramanand advised, we zip between the fourth and fifth pilings from the right bank, safe from the waves breaking over steel girders and concrete beams lost during construction. Crews of men dangle like pupae on threads of jute as they paint the trestles. Huge work barges, the size of football fields, are strung together on the far shore. Most likely they will stay there, mothballed, until the next bridge is built. Several tugs crisscross the river, and each salutes us with a blast of its horn as it passes. The electrical towers are in place, waiting to be strung with the wire coiled in huge spools on the bank. Everyone on and around the bridge looks industrious, but neither Shankar nor I can figure out exactly what they're doing. As soon as someone picks up a tool, he seems to drop it and head off to pick up another one.

Tezpur is called the City of Blood, an epithet it earned as the battleground for gods fighting over the hand of Princess Usha, the loveliest woman on earth. The war raged for years and destroyed the landscape for hundreds of kilometers around Usha's castle. Near her palace, on Manukata Hill, was an altar where human sacrifices were performed. All the gods attended these ceremonies, finding them amusing operatic spectacles. It is said that Shiva was particularly fond of the bloodletting and reserved his favorite spot by pressing his foot deep into Rudraped Rock; the imprint can still be seen today.

Because of the bridge and the many factories here, Tezpur is one of the fastest-growing cities in Assam, and one of the most polluted. I have to open the aperture of my camera three extra stops to compensate for the smog. After docking, Shankar and I walk downtown, dodging traffic and other pedestrians as we go. I lose count of the number of times my toes are trampled. The first twenty minutes are diverting, but after that I long to return to the serene beauty of the Brahmaputra. The river, I realize, has become my home. It's the only place I feel comfortable. Shankar, however, wants to tour the city of blood.

We hire a rickshaw and trundle off to Cole Park, where Princess Usha's castle once stood. While inspecting the ruins of the fourth-century royal palace, I'm besieged by scores of schoolchildren. They all want to touch me. This is fine for the first twenty-five pokes, but as it continues, I begin to wonder whether the sacrificial altar is still in operation. Shankar is also put off by this treatment, and we return quickly to the ghat. Three hours after landing, we're once again humming along with the current.

The paddle feels reassuring in my hands; my fingers now fit snugly into the well-worn grooves. After a while Shankar takes a break, lies back to, as he says, "keep an eye on the clouds." I stroke lazily, pausing to survey the water. Off to starboard a spotbill upends itself to grub in the muck. Nearby a snake-bird cocks its head to spear a frog. Beyond is a row of small whirlpools, each twirling flotsam in endless circles. Ganges dolphins break the surface to grab a lungful of air.

"Wow! Look at that, dude," Shankar exclaims sitting upright and pointing off the bow.

Dead ahead is a bamboo raft that looks as big as a parking lot. Five men are trying to coax it through the shallows. One of the crew wedges a stout pole down the side and tries to lever it forward, but the pole snaps and sends him crashing into the water to a chorus of hoots and cheers. Not one of the crew looks older than twenty.

"Trouble, eh?" Shankar asks after greeting them.

"No, this is how it is," one of them says, pausing for a second to confer with his friends. "What's that?" he adds, waving a finger at me.

"That's a firang. American."

"Ah!" The man smiles. "Where is your jet plane?"

The boys left their hometown, Dibrugarh, almost a month ago. They expect it will take them another two or three weeks to reach Gauhati, where they hope to sell their bamboo.

"Each piece is long and straight, the best in Assam. We will get a good price," the tallest of the group says. "Where are you coming from in that piece of a boat?"

When we tell them, their eyes pop out. Three years ago they heard about a boat leaving Saikhoa Ghat loaded with thatch. The two-man crew was heading for Gauhati.

"Did you see them? Do you know what happened to them?" the one with the broken pole asks.

"No."

"Nobody does. Never saw them again. Crocodiles . . . How many did you see?"

"We have many charms," Shankar boasts.

"They must be powerful. You are still alive."

They believe the stretch of river between Saikhoa Ghat and Dibrugarh is infested with ghosts, evil spirits, burrus, giant turtles, and crocodiles. To a man, they would never consider going above Dibrugarh by boat.

"Why don't you join us. We could use some help."

"No thanks, we're looking for something special," I say.

They ask what it is; I produce the illustration of the pink-headed duck and demonstrate its call.

"Is there a reward?" one of them queries.

"I hope so," I reply.

"What do we do if we see one?"

"Shout as loud as you can. I'll hear you."

Before leaving, we exchange presents. They give us a new bamboo push pole, and I hand them several packs of ciga-rettes. We drift apart, but a hundred yards off, a voice calls after us. One of the boys sprints along the beach. "We need a match! A match, please."

13

The Treasure of Kamali-Kunwari

GAUHATI IS 136 kilometers from Tezpur, a three- to six-day journey depending on weather, currents, and our mood. So far we've averaged thirty-five kilometers a day; true to her name, *Lahey-Lahey* is taking it slow.

Later that week we skim alongside the thick growth of the left bank. Above us a bluff rises straight up from the water, curving twenty-five to thirty feet out over our heads, reminding me of a rogue wave. Many trees in the area have fallen, and their tips overhang the bank. Kingfishers swoop in and out of their nests in the mud cliffs; a flock of widgeons bobs off to starboard, too far away to be disturbed by us. But seconds later, for no apparent reason, the ducks take flight and the kingfishers shriek.

"I'll bet there are turtles around here," Shankar comments, keeping an eye out for the telltale bubbles. "I'm hungry."

A loud cracking noise cuts the air. We stop paddling. Suddenly, with an explosive sound, a giant chunk of the bank drops into the water just twenty yards astern, splattering us with mud. Waves roll over the rail and *Lahey-Lahey* spins out of control, ramming the cliff. Shankar pushes off and we regain steerage. As we frantically try to paddle clear of the bank, we hear another cracking sound, louder and closer.

"Paddle, man. Paddle!" Shankar shouts.

Not more than three boat lengths away, a fissure opens in the bluff and another piece of the cliff begins to teeter. More roots snap; the crack gets wider. *Splam!* The cliff plunges into the river. A tree limb strikes me, and Shankar is buried under a deluge of mud and leaves. *Lahey-Lahey* is pinned, beam to the current, hard against this new island, the bilge filling rapidly. I jump overboard and grab the bailing can.

"Shankar! Shankar!"

"Yeah, yeah, I'm OK."

"Then get out. She's going under. Bail!"

"I can't even stand."

He manages to free himself and clambers over the side. *Lahey-Lahey*'s rail clears the surface, and the two of us get to work, trying to empty the swamped boat before she capsizes. Shankar uses his new shoes to bail. We gain enough freeboard to climb back in, and we paddle to a nearby island safe from nightmare bank. We spread everything out to dry and lie down in the sun, too exhausted to talk.

Later I survey *Lahey-Lahey* for damage. The bottom planks have opened, crazing the protective layer of pitch; the stem has twisted and the topsides are loose along the stern post. Several dozen well-placed nails make her seaworthy again, but I can't stop all the leaks. From here on, for every hour of paddling, we bail for ten minutes. After making an offering to Brahma and imploring Him to watch over us, we head out, keeping our distance from the bank.

As we close in on Gauhati, we begin to see the freighters of the Brahmaputra. They're shaped like arks, with plenty of freeboard, bluff bows, and wide beams. *Lahey-Lahey* is smaller than their rudders. Over fifty feet on the water line, they carry jute, grain, rice, firewood, and other bulk cargos. We watch the crews struggle as they tow or pole their ungainly vessels against the current. On average, traveling upstream takes three times longer than traveling downstream.

The sunset sky is ablaze, the water washed in red. It's clear now why so many Assamese refer to the Brahmaputra by its mythical name of Lohitya, or Red River. According to Assamese legend, Parasuram, an avatar of Ram, hatcheted his evil mother. For this crime, he was condemned to circle the globe with the axe, unable to cleanse himself of his mother's blood. After years of wandering, when he finally reached the Brahmaputra, the holy water purified him; the axe slipped from his hand and the blood dissolved, forever staining the river.

"There they are. Up ahead. Those are the Gauhati Hills," Shankar exclaims the next day.

"Can't be. Look at the map, Shankar. It's Bura Mayang. We're still ten, twelve miles upstream."

"Hey, man, this is my town. I know these hills."

As we come abreast of the hill, it becomes apparent that this is Bura Mayang; my smugness irks Shankar no end.

"At least you're consistent," he notes, "just as poor a winner as a loser."

We continue paddling long after sunset, determined to reach Gauhati that night. There's no moon, and thick clouds obscure the stars, but the city lights guide us. At the edge of town we ship the paddles and glide noiselessly, our eyes on the lit windows along the riverbank. In one a woman cooks dinner alone, pausing to smile at her television; next door a man sits at a table reading a newspaper; the neighbors are arguing; and downstream a young couple embrace and start to disrobe. We float by, undetected, the images changing, lights flicking on and off, people coming and going.

The residential neighborhood gives way to the commercial district. Strings of light bulbs ring a busy marketplace, and headlights bounce along the roads. Solitary figures with oil lamps crouch along the bank, fishing or urinating. A raga sometimes floats through the air; the smell of garlic and onions whets our appetites.

Steering into a state-run ghat, we bang on the side of a dilapidated workboat.

"Who's that?" a voice asks.

"Two travelers," Shankar explains. "Can we tie up for the night?"

Giving him no time to answer, Shankar climbs aboard. He speaks Assamese, and I understand little except that he's calling me an "important American official." Shankar convinces Paresch, the night watchman, to bend the rules and allow us to moor next to the barge. Paresch helps us remove our gear and promises to keep an eye on *Lahey-Lahey*. He pours us tea and proposes a toast: "You both must be crazy to travel in a splinter like that, but welcome anyway."

We walk ashore, and scores of people in the market stop haggling to stare at us.

"What's wrong?" I ask Shankar.

He doesn't know, but we quickly find out with a glimpse of our reflection in a window. We look awful. I haven't shaved in days, and Shankar's hair could be used for a bird's nest. We're dressed for the river, not the metropolis; our pant legs are rolled up, our knotted shirts are open, and we're caked with dirt. We hail a cab and drive straight to Shankar's family home. This time everyone is up when we arrive.

"I'll get some hot water ready," says Kumar, pinching his nose.

"You must be very hungry," adds his mother, bless her heart, who has cooked a large dinner. "A mother always knows when her boy is near." She dotes on us, heaping giant portions on our plates, refusing to let Kumar and Amar question us until we've eaten.

When I first visited Gauhati, after the plane ride from New Delhi, I saw little of the city besides the bus station. This time Shankar has promised to show me the sights. Over the past three weeks, he's been telling me stories about this timeless city, which has been reincarnated often under many names.

Krishna and his white stallion visited here, leaving hoof marks in the granite. Other, lesser gods have also left their astral calling cards, usually in the form of a hand or foot print pressed into stone. A number of temples dedicated to minor deities and fringe cults are located here: the city is the center of the cosmos for Tantrists and many astrologers. Hien Tsang, the Oriental Marco Polo, lavishly praised the city (then named Pragjyotisphur) for its wealth, architecture, and culture. In particular he was impressed by the astrologers, who could read a man's future by studying his shadow.

Earthquakes and floods have destroyed the buildings Hien Tsang wrote about in the sixth century; however, in some pockets of the city ancient traditions and culture remain intact. I want to meet someone in touch with this past, hoping they might know about the pink-headed duck. Shankar recommends Kamakhya Temple as a place to visit, saying, "They still do things the old way."

In the morning Shankar and I decide to climb the hundreds of stone steps leading to the temple complex on Nilachal Hill. The four stairways (one on each side of the hill for each of the seasons) were built in a single night by King Narakaur, a mortal who dared to love a goddess. One step from completing his labor of love, he was tricked by the goddess and smitten dead for his arrogance.

I pause at each landing to catch my breath and study the statuary of penises and vaginas which are intended to inspire the weary. Kamakhya is, after all, dedicated to the forces of creation. It honors Kali and her *yoni,* or vagina, as the supreme creative principle, and it extols the sexual prowess of Shiva, who, from the look of things, was very well endowed.

When Kali's breast fell upstream to form Majuli, her vagina landed here in Gauhati and created Nilachal Hill. Tantrists have been gathering here for centuries. To them, any land within sight of the hill is sacred, and no higher moment exists in this illusory life than sexual climax within the aura of Kali's yoni.

At the top of the stairway, we're greeted by a dozen priests all waiting to guide visitors. The fifteen hundred devotees living in the complex earn their keep by working as instructors in the rituals a pilgrim can perform to expiate sin. We avoid hiring a guide, but I do buy the freedom of a dove, the cheapest available sacrifice. The priest, or *panda,* dabs the head of the bird with a mixture of saffron and water. As he releases it, the panda raises his voice in prayer.

"Oh, Mother of Creation, bless this man. Grace him with many children."

"Hey, I don't want many children."

"It's the usual prayer . . . You will have to buy two more animals: one to ask the goddess to forget and the other to ask her to listen again."

The temple of Kamakhya is a sprawling building, with distinct sections built at different times. The architecture is a jumble of corners, domes, circles, spires, and arches. Some of the walls are weathered and smooth; others are decorated with filigree and statuary. Most of the relief work celebrates genitalia; doorways are arched and crowned with escutcheons emblazoned with mating animals; fountains are shaped like vaginas. Shankar tells me that in the temple basement there's a tunnel connecting this shrine of the yoni to Shillong, a city nearly a hundred miles away.

Shankar wanders off to take pictures, while I join the line of pilgrims waiting to enter the temple. Fifteen minutes later I slip away from the crowd, leave the main chamber, and head for what I suspect are the basement stairs. Two steps from the bottom my sleuthing is abruptly stopped by a surprisingly burly panda.

"What are you doing?" he demands.

"Looking for the passage, the tunnel of love."

"How dare you! Only true believers can come down here. Go now!" he shouts.

"Are you making a sacrifice?" another panda asks, as I walk inside a nearby pavilion.

"I made one near the entrance," I say, a bit confused.

"Are you here for the slaughter?"

"Pardon me?"

"Leave this holy place. Go away."

"Can I take some pictures first?"

"You insult the gods. Go!"

Other pandas are attracted by the commotion and circle me, wagging their fingers and scorning me in low voices. Luckily I spot Shankar in the stone amphitheater overlooking the pavilion. I apologize profusely to the pandas, explaining that I'm a firang and intend no disrespect. I join Shankar, who's watching a middle-aged couple lead a goat into a small enclosure. They give the leash to a stout-legged priest who ties the animal's legs and positions its head on a chopping block. Another priest pins the goat as his partner raises the largest cleaver I've ever seen; the head must be severed in one blow. The executioner grunts as he lifts the heavy weapon. "Haaar!"

Blood spurts from the neck, dousing the panda, and the head drops to the floor. The body twitches as it's stuffed inside a plastic bag; one leg punctures the plastic and the priest shoves it back inside. The executioner waves the couple out and swings the bag over a half wall. No doubt goat will be on the menu tonight.

Another couple enters leading two goats. I leave immediately and walk over to the Pond of Fortune, a kinder locale. A priest tells me that Indra, mother goddess, dug the pond for Sati, an avatar of Kali. He swears that the pond is bottomless and claims that scientists trying to plumb its depths have never struck bottom.

"It begins on the other side of the world," he states matter-of-factly.

Less than a stone's throw away is a small pool dedicated to Shiva, and it's full of turtles. I pick one of them up and try to coax its leathery head out of the shell. A man dressed in white approaches me. Assuming he's going to scold me for doing something sacrilegious, I drop the reptile back into the water.

"Good morning," the man says in perfect English. "Do you like turtles? They are holy to Shiva, but you must know that, don't you?"

I introduce myself as a tourist with much to learn.

"That, my foreign friend, is obvious. Many priests would beat you if they saw you handling the holy turtles."

"Oh, then you're not a priest?"

"I am a Tantrika following the Tantric Way."

He has been watching me and the reactions of the pandas. "They think you might be an evil spirit. Did you do something to offend them?"

"I don't know."

"I think you need help. If you like, I will teach you," he offers, pausing to look at the sun. "Yes, you have been sent to me for instruction. I can tell."

For a moment, his words and gestures remind me of my old friend Babba in Calcutta. This man, however, has never left Assam.

"This is where I will remain. I will live and die here among my brothers. I want my ashes scattered on the yoni, and only my brothers know the rites."

"What rites?"

"Secrets," he says softly, seating himself at the edge of the pond.

"Can I learn them?"

"Certainly, but you must study and prepare yourself . . . People, you see, don't understand us very well," he says, pondering the water. Two turtles leave the pond and head slowly toward us. "People are ignorant about Tantrists. They think we are evil because we celebrate sex . . . sex is a way to god."

I'm all ears. The notion of salvation through orgasm has its appeal. Shankar joins us, and the two men from Assam speak rapidly.

"This guy's off his rocker," Shankar tells me, switching from Assamese to English.

"Oh, you speak English as well," the Tantrika says, surprising my friend.

I explain to Shankar that the man is willing to show us how to reach the Source of All Light through sexual activity. Shankar is momentarily intrigued until the Tantrika reminds us that arduous study is necessary.

"It will take years for you to discover the answer," he says. "I will answer as many questions as I can, but there are very strict guidelines I must follow."

"Are you going to stay?" Shankar asks me.

"Yes, maybe there are shortcuts."

"Good luck. I'm going back to town. Do you remember where the house is? . . . Good. I'll see you later or at the boat in the morning. We leave at . . ."

"Ten. We leave at ten," I answer, "unless you want to stay longer."

"I'll be ready. See you later, alligator."

"May Shiva enter your heart," bids the Tantrika.

We sit in the same spot for an hour. He explains that Tantrists view the libido as the essence of the universe. To him, sexual energy is the purest form of energy. If properly directed, sex and ecstasy provide a path to Nirvana.

"Orgasm is bliss," he instructs. "Orgasm is the point of nothingness. It is the only moment when the human no longer desires."

He's got a point.

"Orgasm is the ultimate state of desirelessness, something we call *moksa* or *anada.*"

The Tantrika's name is Prem Sarma. He's forty years old, although he looks sixty. Thick brows shade his recessed eyes, and his beard fans out across his thin chest. He grew up in Shillong, the third of five sons, and learned English at one of the elite missionary schools. After finishing college, he worked as a teacher.

"Years ago, during a term vacation, I met a very holy man on a visit to Kamakhya. At the end of the semester I left my job. I left everything to become his pupil . . . to be a Tantrika and find bliss."

"Has it worked out?"

"Better than I hoped. I love life. Look at me, I am very happy."

Assam is one of the few places in the world a Tantrist can find happiness. Not only is it home to Kali's yoni, but the people are tolerant; some of the rites peculiar to cults within Tantrism are outlawed in other states of India. Even here, he says he's stared at when he wears his weights.

Weights?

"Yes, it is an exercise in self-control. I will show you."

Prem demonstrates by taking out two iron sash weights, each about three pounds, that he carries in a satchel on his belt. Making sure that none of the pandas are watching, he stands and attaches the weights to the tip of his penis. This exercise in self-control looks incredibly painful.

"But I feel only good things . . . It is something we learn. You can learn its pleasure."

"No thanks. I want to know more about moksa."

I find it impossible to concentrate with the weights dangling in front of me and ask if he would mind removing them. As he unties the cord, he talks about the benefits of the Tantric life. "We seek to enjoy, others do not."

Most high-caste Hindus equate the loss of semen with a loss of spiritual power. Indeed, Brahmins consider Tantrists unbalanced sex fiends, polluting themselves and everything that is holy by their rituals. For Brahmins, self-denial is requisite to finding peace.

"And that is wrong," says Prem. "Why should you or I deny our bodies? Why not put them to work? Why not use sexual energy to reach moksa? I believe god is in the pleasures of life, not pain."

Instead of suppressing pleasure in its many forms, he has

studied methods of channeling and enhancing these sensa-
tions. Pivotal is the notion that a man can exist beyond the
realm of physical sensation once he has learned to internalize
his sexual encounters. Many Tantric rituals involve stimulants
such as liquor and drugs, which, when used properly, extend
the state of moksa. It's a highly regimented existence, with the
sacred text of the Tantras dictating tasks to be accomplished
each day. Prem remains tight-lipped when I ask about certain
Tantric rituals, like their fabled orgies.

"Secrets," he repeats.

"Who can tell me?"

"My teacher."

He talks a little about his teacher, and I share the story of
the pink-headed duck. After another hour of talking, he agrees
to mention the pink duck to his mentor, and in exchange I will
buy him a meal. As we leave the temple grounds, he starts
calling me "pupil." We take a taxi to a little restaurant with
no furniture. The food is served on plantain leaves and the tea
in gourds. We squat against a wall, eating with our fingers, as
he talks about the way to harness the sexual animal and ride
its power. When we finish, Prem refuses a cigarette; instead
he opens a small bag that is tied around his neck. Inside are
various narcotics.

"Try this one. It is much better than tobacco."

"What is it?"

"A piece of happiness."

Unwilling to turn down happiness, I thank him and we head
to a neighborhood park, where we sit in the shade of a giant
sal tree. We talk until words become nearly impossible for me
and I just sit there, gazing happily at the grass. At some later
point Prem excuses himself, saying he must return to his
teacher. I'm content to stay put. He will be back after asking
if I can attend the meeting of his group scheduled for that
night.

I awake from my dreams as dusk falls. Several cups of tea

chase away the grogginess. It has been four hours since Prem left, so I decide to move on. In the distance I can see the lights of a Ferris wheel spinning above the treetops. I start walking toward it when I hear Prem's voice. He's running after me.

"Hold on . . . Wait!" he gasps. "I have good news . . . My teacher has said yes. He wants to meet you and see the bird you carry in your bag. Tonight, after my brothers meet, you will see him."

We head east in a cab and get out at the base of Chitrachel Hill, the site of the Nabagraha Temple, or Shrine of the Nine Planets. This is the seat of Assamese astrological study. Many years ago, before rich patrons lured the priests away from the temple to be personal astrologers, Nabagraha was famous throughout the Orient. Chinese, Burmese, Thai, and Hindu pilgrims waited in long lines to learn their futures.

A monkey darts across my path as I start to climb the temple steps.

"No. This way. Follow me," Prem signals, opening the gate of a cemetery across the street, one of the graveyards established by the British during World War II. We walk past headstones inscribed with the names Campbell, Scott, Thayer, Smith, and Glennon.

It has grown quite dark, and several oil lamps are flickering in a corner of the cemetery. Prem pulls me gently by the sleeve. Three or four people are standing in the shadows and others seem to be sitting in a circle. We're too far away to see them clearly. As we walk toward them, a voice calls out and Prem stops. Ordering me not to move, he takes the illustration of the pink-headed duck and slips off, leaving me at the tombstone of Corporal Michael Wright. After a few minutes I hear the gate latch open again. Three figures are heading directly for me; two of them are supporting a third who appears to be drunk and is dressed, head to foot, in muslin.

One of the men shouts in Assamese; Prem, far behind me, responds. There's a grunt, and the trio veers quickly away. As they do, the shrouded drunk slumps to the ground. The men start to drag him by the feet. As his head thumps on a stone marker, I instinctively step forward to help.

"Hey, watch out for his head. Slow down! I'll help you," I say as I catch up to them and lift the drunk by the shoulders.

The other two men begin shouting, one yelling at me while his friend calls to Prem and his group.

"I'm only trying to help," I tell them.

The drunk's head snaps back. The cloth slips and I feel cold skin in my grip. My stomach churns; I'm holding a female corpse. Prem grabs my arm. The Tantrikas speak excitedly before Prem leads me away.

"I told you not to move . . . You were not supposed to see that. The master is very upset. It is all my fault . . ."

"Just get my picture back," I plead.

I was prepared to drink wine from a skull; I had imagined partaking of mind-altering drugs; I had even wished to observe one of the Tantrists' fabled orgies, but necrophilia holds no interest for me.

Prem goes to get the picture. Five minutes pass, then ten. Picture or no picture, I'm ready to leave.

"Prem," I shout.

"Coming."

At last he returns, saying, "My teacher would like to meet you tomorrow. He wants to explain what you saw. He wants you to understand . . ."

"Where's the picture?"

"Here."

"I'm going," I say, clicking on my flashlight. The beam strikes the hem of his shirt. "Are you all right?" I ask, startled by the bloodstain.

"Top of the world, thank you," he says lowering his hands to cover the splotch. For a split second, his shirttail moves to one side, exposing his bloodied groin.

I spin away. As I fling open the gate, he calls, "See you at the temple tomorrow, same time?"

Out on the street, shivering, I head for the workboat. Paresch is surprised to see me. He leads me to our gear on the main deck and waits until I've rolled out my bedding, then he pulls up a chair and starts asking questions about America. He's on night duty and wants company. In the hope that he will leave me in peace, I take out my last wrist radio and present it to him. We're both amazed to hear music. It's the first time one of the micro radios has actually picked up a station. He heads to the upper deck for better reception.

Before morning tea I buy a newspaper. Half of the front page is dedicated to the GNLF. Fighting is at a peak; scores of soldiers on both sides have been injured or killed. Also on the front page is a report from Dhaka, Bangladesh, where student demonstrations have disrupted most government services. If the civil unrest increases, we may have to cancel our plans to paddle into the Bay of Bengal.

"Did you have fun last night?" Shankar asks, arriving a few minutes early.

"Do me a favor, just get in the boat."

"Don't you want to stay another day or two?"

"Let's go."

"What happened to you?"

"I'll tell you later."

"Well, I had a great time. Went to a restaurant. Saw a movie. Went to . . ."

We clear Gauhati, avoiding the ferries and giving plenty of room to tugs hauling barges. The river traffic increases even more as we draw abeam of Pandu, once a pleasant suburb and now an undistinguished urban sprawl. Ahead is the Pandu railroad bridge. A freight train, its steam engine a survivor from another era, is creeping across the heavily trussed span. The red stack belches thick coal smoke. Streams of people move in both directions on the pedestrian lanes of the bridge. Near the middle almost everyone pauses to say a short prayer and make an offering to the river god.

Plink! Poink! . . . Coins hit the water all around us. In India travelers pay their toll to the gods. If they forget, something awful may happen during the journey to remind them. A donation to the first needy person in sight is an acceptable penance. People start using us as a target. *Splash! Plink! Clunk!* A coin ricochets around the bilge.

"Put your hat on and start paddling," Shankar urges. "They're starting to zero in."

Stratus clouds are gathering, and it's not long before the sun is completely obscured. A northeast wind kicks up, gusting above thirty knots. It starts to drizzle, and visibility drops to less than a quarter of a mile. The steadily increasing wind churns the river into a cauldron of milky spume. Whitecaps rise. This is the first storm of our trip, and the first time we wish for a bigger boat. With so little freeboard, we ship water any time a wave strikes forward of the stern quarter. The rough motion stresses the planks, and *Lahey-Lahey* starts leaking like a sieve.

The river is no longer talking to us, it's shouting. We start surfing, riding the crests of the larger waves, trying not to broach. The boat races along as we hover on the line between exhilaration and disaster. All the other unmotorized craft are beached, waiting for the storm to pass. Even here, on the most densely populated segment of the river, the Brahmaputra has become ours alone. We hug the weather shore, pushing *Lahey-Lahey* to her limits. For today, Shankar calls me skipper.

"I sure hope you know what you're doing, Skip."

"No problem. Just keep bailing."

"Didn't you lose a boat once?"

"Keep bailing."

Just below Pandu the Brahmaputra squeezes into a narrow channel and then spreads out as if sprayed from a nozzle. The banks recede and islands rise up. We go wherever the wind pushes us; as long as the waves remain off the stern, we're doing the right thing.

Sometime during the night the front moves through. We awake on our desert island to a cloudless sky dotted with swooping birds. We have no idea where we are or how many miles we've traveled. On a nearby island, larger than ours, a spiral of smoke draws our attention. Twenty minutes later we join a trio of thatch cutters. The leader is fifteen years old and the other two are his younger brothers. Like the fishermen, they pay a heavy tax on their harvest (30 percent), but they have the optimism of youth.

"We are going to be the maharajas of thatch . . . When we are rich, we will visit you in America."

They tell us we've already passed Hajo, the one spot in Assam considered holy by Buddhists, Hindus, and, remarkably, Muslims. The Islamic shrine at Paomecca was built over bags of earth brought from Mecca, and visiting it bestows one fourth the blessing of a trip to Islam's holiest shrine. Buddhists believe Lord Gautama came to Hajo, although the historical record makes no mention of it. Cult members point to a sacred rock believed to be a piece of butter dropped by the Great One. Hindus crowd the temples built alongside the footprints of Shiva and Brahma.

The thatch cutters say that Bartala is across the river. If we keep to the right bank, we should reach Lehi by midafternoon. I show them the picture of the pink-headed duck.

"I don't know it," says the oldest brother. "Are you sure it's around here?"

"Yes."

"Have you seen it?"

"Probably many times," I say with conviction.

"Huh?" Shankar interjects.

"Sure! We've seen it. We just didn't notice it."

The thatch cutters walk us to the boat, and as we pull away, they shout, "Gūlāb-sīr! Gūlāb-sīr! Gūlāb-sīr . . ."

Not far downstream we encounter a fleet of large boats grounded by the storm. Crews from most of the boats work together, freeing one keel at a time. We stop to lend a hand, joining a gang of almost forty-five men dragging a fully loaded freighter through the shallows. These men refuse to help two other vessels that are owned by bongs, sailors from Bangladesh. The Indians would rather spit on a bong boat than help it, no matter what the predicament. The hospitality of the river is for Indians and their invited guests only.

"Every meter from here to Dhubri is infested with bongs. Watch out! They steal and cheat and destroy and . . ." one captain tells us.

We dismiss his warning. So far the few bongs we've met have been dull and timid. If anything, they've proved the least threatening of all the groups on the river. Above Gauhati we found them grouped in small communities that judiciously kept their distance from the others. They're all business — not once has a bong offered us tea.

One thing is apparent: the closer we get to the border of Bangladesh, the more people are camped along the river's edge. The jungle recedes, animal tracks are few, and even birds become scarce. Kingfishers, usually plentiful, are now a rare sight. Small huts line the banks, and fishing nets reach out from every spit. Three days after leaving Gauhati, we lose any sense of solitude. There are people everywhere we look, competing with nature and each other.

We stop at two bong villages for tea. As usual, people at the ghat help us moor *Lahey-Lahey,* but nobody will answer questions. Looks of fear cross the villagers' faces whenever I start writing in my notebook. They think I'm a government official who will have them deported. At the tea shops we're forced to pay in advance.

"The Hindus come and eat and never pay afterward. If I do not know you, I demand money first . . . What else can I do? The police will not listen to me," says one shop owner.

He tells us that he left Bangladesh illegally twelve years ago. India is hell to him, but Bangladesh was worse. Misery, he tells us, is his constant companion.

"I have slept in the street . . . lost family to floods, wars, and famines. My life is one of many tears . . ."

Hardship is one thing he can rely on, he says. Nothing has ever been given to him, so he's reluctant to share. Even smiles are hoarded. He assures us that his faith keeps him going, adding, "What else is there?"

The riverfront is one of the few places where he and other refugees are allowed to live. None of the Hindus want this land, he tells us. "Why would they? Floods destroy our houses and drown our cattle . . . Still, it is somewhere."

As we continue down the river, it becomes impossible to find an empty island. Any island with vegetation has dozens of people living on it, and even on the bare sandbars there are bong fishing camps. In the past four days we've spotted only one osprey; we haven't seen a stork, an eagle, or a duck. In the marshes are only crows, herons, and swallows.

"Do you think it's too late to find the duck?" Shankar asks as we head into the smog of Goalpara's factories.

"That depends on whether the duck's a Muslim."

When we stop in Goalpara for lunch, we eat quickly and push on. We've lost our desire to explore cities. Below Goalpara the once pristine Brahmaputra is a river of filth. No longer can we scoop up a handful of water and drink it. Raw sewage and brown scum string out in mile-long slicks, and the murky water surface no longer reflects light. Paddling becomes a chore, and I suddenly feel cut off from the river.

At Jalasar Ghat the owner of the ferry connecting this port with Dhubri puts us up for the night, but warns us that it would be better to move on. "Only mosquitoes like it here."

It's a few minutes before six that evening when we stroll into the Jalasar market. I'm examining some shirts when a bell chimes the hour. *Whap!* A clerk snatches the cotton from my hand and ushers me out of the shop. They're closing for the day. Several doors away I hear someone shouting at Shankar, ordering him out of the store. He wants to buy something, but the owner won't let him and raises a stick, threatening him.

The only place still open is a tea shop with about twenty men inside, all with scraggly beards and fezlike hats. One man approaches us, and Shankar speaks to him in an unfamiliar Bengali dialect, explaining that we want dinner.

"Impossible. All shops are closed."

It becomes clear that this is a community of devout Muslims who don't want trouble and don't like outsiders. We return to the ghat to cook our own meal: rice, dal, and radishes yet again.

The next morning, after a night of mosquito attacks, the ferry captain offers to tow *Lahey-Lahey* across the river on his run to Dhubri. This will save us a full day of paddling through sludge, so we accept. We join the captain as he strides to the bow to make his offering to the river god.

On this ferry the men are allowed the comfort and view of the upper deck, while the women ride on the main deck with the livestock.

"Don't you Americans know anything? This is the way it must be done . . . Men here and women there. You must read the Koran," one passenger informs me.

I wander about, looking for friendly faces. A soldier is reading a newspaper, and I ask to borrow a section. Shankar translates the lead story about rioting in Dhaka. Martial law has been declared in Bangladesh and the border is closed. Shankar and I decide to curtail our trip at Dhubri, the last town in India on the Brahmaputra.

A contingent of Dhubri policemen meets us at the ferry ghat. Once again the information network has monitored our movements. This time, however, the officer in charge shakes our hands, congratulating us on a successful voyage. As far as he knows, we are the first to paddle the length of the Brahmaputra from Burma to Bangladesh.

"Well done," the officer says, patting me on the back. "Ah, yes, before I forget, I have a letter for you."

A letter? For me? There's no return address. Before I open the envelope, the policeman asks if we're planning to continue down the river. He's relieved to hear our decision.

"The bongs are firing on everyone heading south. They think that only dissidents and troublemakers are crossing the border," he says before asking us one last question: "What are you going to do with the boat?"

"Sell her," I tell him.

"What?" Shankar asks.

"What else are we going to do with her? Let's auction her off right now."

Shankar rises to the occasion. Mimicking a huckster's voice, he gathers a crowd. The policemen step back as we watch Shankar display his powers of salesmanship.

"Gather round. Look at this fine yacht . . . This is the chance of a lifetime. Own a piece of history. It's your chance to . . ."

Three men start poking at *Lahey-Lahey*'s sides, digging their knives into her planks. I step between them and the boat. At the very least *Lahey-Lahey* has earned respect.

"What do I hear for this fine craft . . . Give me a price . . ."

"Fifty rupees!"

"Fifty and fifty paises."

"Fifty-one."

"Fifty-one-fifty."

Shankar and I huddle. "All right," he booms, "this is your lucky day. The firang wants you to be happy. A hundred rupees [a little less than seven dollars] takes this splendid craft, made with love, made with . . ."

"Sold! One hundred!" yells a fisherman holding the note in his hand.

He gets the boat, but without my paddle, which I'm determined to take home. My blankets fetch fifty rupees apiece, but no one wants our pots, pans, and bowls. The kerosene lantern brings ten rupees, and the tent nets us five more. In all, we realize a grand sixteen dollars.

The auction over, we look around town, feeling empty. The river trip is over. *Lahey-Lahey* belongs to a stranger. We search for a bar, but Dhubri is dry; we can't even buy liquor in the black market district. Eventually we end up at the railway station, waiting in silence for the next train to Gauhati. Five hours after landing in Dhubri, we climb aboard the mail train for the overnight trip to the state capital.

"Well, it's really over now, eh?" Shankar remarks as we leave the station.

"Maybe not. There are still a few days left on my visa, and I've got a couple of ideas. How about going to Kadali with me?" I ask. Kadali is the site of the treasure of Kamala-Kunwari, the legendary Amazon of Assam, who led an all-female army that trounced all male comers. She is said to have established a matriarchate that controlled central Assam for several generations.

"What about the curse?" he asks, reminding me that the legend promises death to any man who looks upon Kamala-Kunwari's treasure chest.

"My charms will protect us."

"You have the charms, my friend — you go and look for her treasure and I'll meet you in Delhi."

I reach into my bag for the map. As I spread it out, the unopened letter falls to the floor.

"Jeez, I almost forgot . . . Hey, Shankar, read this."

The letter is from Tamuli and his message is short: "I think I saw a pink-headed duck today. You should come here if you are still looking . . . Your friend, Tamuli of Salmora."

"Well, what do you think?" Shankar asks.

"I'm thinking about pink-headed ducks. They're not extinct, just hard to find . . . I'm going back upriver, do you want to come along?"

Afterword

What's next for me? A journey through air, perhaps. I'm intrigued by the notion of meandering in the jet stream, floating nonstop around the world. Leave from Brooklyn and take the long way to Manhattan.

At lift-off, the same people who helped me in previous journeys will be there. At this point we're a team. Virginia Reath and Jim Angell will be nearby, aided by Ike Williams, Steve Huff, Harry Foster, Dave Rottner, Peg Anderson, Dr. Kevin Cahill, and my family.